Common Core Connections
Language Arts
Grade 5

Carson-Dellosa Publishing, LLC
Greensboro, North Carolina

Credits
Content Editor: Nancy Rogers Bosse
Copy Editor: Karen Seberg

Visit *carsondellosa.com* for correlations to Common Core, state, national, and Canadian provincial standards.

Carson-Dellosa Publishing, LLC
PO Box 35665
Greensboro, NC 27425 USA
carsondellosa.com

ISBN 978-1-62442-796-1

03-096151151

Table of Contents

Introduction 4

Common Core State Standards Alignment Matrix 5

Skill Assessment 7

Skill Assessment Analysis 11

Reading Standards for Literature 12

Reading Standards for Informational Text 28

Reading Standards: Foundational Skills... 48

Writing Standards 59

Language Standards 76

Answer Key... 91

Introduction

What are the Common Core State Standards for Language Arts?

The standards are a shared set of expectations for each grade level in the areas of reading, writing, speaking, listening, and language. They define what students should understand and be able to do. The standards are designed to be more rigorous and allow for students to justify their thinking. They reflect the knowledge that is necessary for success in college and beyond.

As described in the Common Core State Standards, students who master the standards in reading, writing, speaking, listening, and language as they advance through the grades will exhibit the following capabilities:

1. They demonstrate independence.
2. They build strong content knowledge.
3. They respond to the varying demands of audience, task, purpose, and discipline.
4. They comprehend as well as critique.
5. They value evidence.
6. They use technology and digital media strategically and capably.
7. They come to understand other perspectives and cultures.*

How to Use This Book

This book is a collection of practice pages aligned to the Common Core State Standards for English Language Arts and appropriate for fifth grade. Included is a skill matrix so that you can see exactly which standards are addressed on the practice pages. Also included are a skill assessment and a skill assessment analysis. Use the assessment at the beginning of the year or at any time of year you wish to assess your students' mastery of certain standards. The analysis connects each test item to a practice page or set of practice pages so that you can review skills with students who struggle in certain areas.

© Carson-Dellosa • CD-104612

Common Core State Standards* Alignment Matrix

Pages	12	13	14	15	16	17	18	19	20	21	22	23	24	25	26	27	28	29	30	31	32	33	34	35	36	37	38	39	40	41	42	43	44	45	46	47	48	49	50	51
5.RL.1		•								•																														
5.RL.2						•		•								•																								
5.RL.3								•		•					•																									
5.RL.4	•																																							
5.RL.5				•																																				
5.RL.6														•		•																								
5.RL.7						•																																		
5.RL.9												•																												
5.RL.10			•		•		•		•		•		•		•																							•	•	•
5.RI.1																		•		•																				
5.RI.2																	•								•															
5.RI.3																						•																		
5.RI.4																										•														
5.RI.5																																			•					
5.RI.6																														•										
5.RI.7																																•								
5.RI.8																							•																	
5.RI.9																																				•				
5.RI.10																	•	•	•		•		•		•		•		•		•		•		•					
5.RF.3																																								
5.RF.3a																																								
5.RF.4																																					•	•	•	•
5.RF.4a																																						•		•
5.RF.4b																																					•	•	•	
5.RF.4c																																					•			
5.W.1																																								
5.W.1a																																								
5.W.1b																																								
5.W.1c																																								
5.W.1d																																								
5.W.2																																								
5.W.2a																																								
5.W.2b																																								
5.W.2c																																								
5.W.2d																																								
5.W.2e																																								
5.W.3																																								
5.W.3a																																								
5.W.3b																																								
5.W.3c																																								
5.W.3d																																								
5.W.3e																																								
5.W.4																																								
5.W.5																																								
5.W.6																																								
5.W.7																																								
5.W.8																																								
5.W.9																																								
5.W.9a																																								
5.W.9b																																								
5.W.10																																								
5.L.1																																								
5.L.1a																																								
5.L.1b																																								
5.L.1c																																								
5.L.1d																																								
5.L.1e																																								
5.L.2																																								
5.L.2a																																								
5.L.2b																																								
5.L.2c																																								
5.L.2d																																								
5.L.2e																																								
5.L.3				•																																				
5.L.3a																																								
5.L.3b				•																																				
5.L.4														•				•										•												
5.L.4a														•				•										•												
5.L.4b																																								
5.L.4c																																								
5.L.5																								•																•
5.L.5a																								•																•
5.L.5b																																								
5.L.5c																																								
5.L.6																																								

© Carson-Dellosa • CD-104612

Common Core State Standards*
Alignment Matrix

Pages	52	53	54	55	56	57	58	59	60	61	62	63	64	65	66	67	68	69	70	71	72	73	74	75	76	77	78	79	80	81	82	83	84	85	86	87	88	89	90
5.RL.1																																							
5.RL.2																																							
5.RL.3																																							
5.RL.4																																							
5.RL.5		•																																					
5.RL.6																																							
5.RL.7																																							
5.RL.9																																							
5.RL.10																																							
5.RI.1																																							
5.RI.2																																							
5.RI.3																																							
5.RI.4																																							
5.RI.5																																							
5.RI.6																																							
5.RI.7																																							
5.RI.8																																							
5.RI.9																																							
5.RI.10																																							
5.RF.3				•	•	•																																	
5.RF.3a				•	•	•																																	
5.RF.4	•	•	•		•	•																																	
5.RF.4a		•																																					
5.RF.4b	•				•																																		
5.RF.4c			•				•																																
5.W.1																		•	•																				
5.W.1a																		•																					
5.W.1b																		•																					
5.W.1c																				•																			
5.W.1d																		•																					
5.W.2																					•		•																
5.W.2a																					•																		
5.W.2b																					•																		
5.W.2c																								•															
5.W.2d																					•																		
5.W.2e																								•															
5.W.3							•	•	•	•	•	•		•																									
5.W.3a														•																									
5.W.3b								•	•	•																													
5.W.3c						•																																	
5.W.3d									•	•	•																												
5.W.3e												•																											
5.W.4							•																																
5.W.5																•			•			•																	
5.W.6																•			•																				
5.W.7																						•																	
5.W.8																						•																	
5.W.9														•								•																	
5.W.9a														•																									
5.W.9b																						•																	
5.W.10																•			•				•																
5.L.1																								•	•	•		•	•	•									
5.L.1a																								•	•	•													
5.L.1b																												•											
5.L.1c																												•											
5.L.1d																														•									
5.L.1e																														•									
5.L.2																									•	•					•	•	•	•					
5.L.2a																									•						•								
5.L.2b																									•							•							
5.L.2c																								•	•														
5.L.2d																																	•						
5.L.2e																																		•					
5.L.3																																						•	
5.L.3a																																			•			•	
5.L.3b																																			•				
5.L.4				•																															•	•			
5.L.4a																																							
5.L.4b				•																																			
5.L.4c																																				•			
5.L.5																																				•	•		•
5.L.5a																																							
5.L.5b																																							•
5.L.5c																																				•	•		
5.L.6								•																															

© Carson-Dellosa • CD-104612

Read the story. Then, answer the questions.

Just Desserts

Jeremy lived with his elderly grandmother. Jeremy arrived at his grandmother's house unwillingly at first. But, now he knew it was a perfect arrangement for both of them—just like milk and cookies, his grandmother would say. His grandmother was a kind woman who loved and cared for Jeremy now that he was alone. She was able to provide him with a roof over his head and food for his belly. Jeremy was able to help his grandmother with the chores around the house that she could no longer do. One of those chores was berry picking.

Jeremy kept thinking about fresh berry pie as he worked. His arms and legs were scratched from the branches and thorns. He did not especially like the bugs, and his arms were becoming weary from the lifting. Picking blackberries was really hard work, but Jeremy knew that it would be worth it when he had his piece of pie!

1. Why did Jeremy live with his grandmother?

    _____

2. Circle the sentence that best describes the theme of the story.
    A. Helping the elderly has its benefits.
    B. Work first, then play.
    C. A good relationship is good for both people.
    D. Be kind to each other.

3. How are Jeremy and his grandmother alike? How are they different?

    _____

4. What does Jeremy's grandmother compare their arrangement to?

    _____

5. How is this story organized?
    A. by cause and effect
    B. chronologically
    C. with an introduction and supporting details
    D. by importance

6. How would this story be different if Jeremy were telling it?

    _____

7. What does the word *unwillingly* mean in the first paragraph?
    A. without trying
    B. reluctantly
    C. happily
    D. by force

8. What does the word *weary* mean in the second paragraph?
    A. tired
    B. strong
    C. tanned
    D. sleepy

Read the passage. Then, answer the questions.

Writing in Ancient Egypt

The ancient Egyptians used an advanced system of writing. Only scribes knew how to write. They developed a form of writing that used pictures and symbols. It was called *hieroglyphics*. Hieroglyphics were often carved on walls or on slabs of stone.

The ancient Egyptians were the first to make paper. They used a reed, called papyrus. They cut the stem of the papyrus into thin slices. They laid some pieces lengthwise and placed others across them. Next, they moistened the layers with water, put a heavy weight on the layers to press them together, and dried them. When the layers were dry, they stuck together in a sheet. The Egyptians rubbed the dried sheet until it was smooth and ready to write on. Sometimes, sheets were joined together to make long scrolls. We get the word *paper* from the word *papyrus*.

9. Circle the main idea of the passage.
   A. The ancient Egyptians were one of the first advanced civilizations.
   B. The ancient Egyptians left behind many clues to tell about their culture.
   C. Writing has been around for a long time.
   D. The ancient Egyptians invented a writing system.

10. Were the ancient Egyptians literate people? Cite at least two facts from the passage to support your answer.

_____

11. Circle how the ancient Egyptians' writing has influenced our writing today.
    A. We use the same alphabet as the Egyptians.
    B. We got the idea of paper from the Egyptians.
    C. We use mostly papyrus to make our paper today.
    D. Only scribes in our society know how to write.

12. What are *hieroglyphics*?
    A. people who know how to read and write
    B. a form of writing that uses pictures and symbols
    C. another name for the ancient Egyptians
    D. a type of paper made from papyrus

13. Using various sources for information, explain what caused the Egyptians to make paper from papyrus.

_____

14. Where could you find more information about ancient Egyptian writing?

_____

15. Write a sentence that includes a conjunction, a preposition, and an interjection.

_____

16. Cross out the incorrect verbs. Then, write the sentence using the correct verbs.
    Chris hoped to see his favorite athlete in person since the day he seen him on TV.

_____

17. Complete the sentence with the correct correlative conjunctions.

    _____ the father _____ his son had ever run a
    marathon before.

18. Rewrite the sentence, inserting commas as needed.
    Wow your garden has tomatoes zucchini corn and carrots growing in it Stephen.

_____

19. Rewrite the sentence to show the correct punctuation.
    I wrote a story called My Life as a Chair.

_____

20. Use a conjunction to combine the two sentences into one sentence.
    Tree frogs sleep during the day. They hunt for food at night.

_____

21. Divide the underlined word into syllables. Then, write its meaning on the line.
    The student <u>misinterpreted</u> the instructions and completed the assignment incorrectly.

_____

22. Underline the idiom in the sentence. Then, write its meaning on the line.
    Sometimes my little brother drives me crazy.

_____

23. Rewrite the sentence, correcting the spelling errors. Use a dictionary if needed.
    The privat proprety belongs to that counselman over their.

_____

24. Circle the meaning of the underlined word.
    <u>Weirs,</u> nets, traps, hooks, and spears were used to catch fish.

    A. American Indians   B. tools used for catching fish
    C. boats   D. women

25. Rewrite the sentence to make it more interesting.
    Brooke likes to ice-skate.

_____

26. Write an opinion essay about your favorite book, movie, TV show, or game. Be sure your essay includes these parts:

- an introduction
- reasons supported by facts
- words that link ideas (for example, *first, finally, next, another*)
- a conclusion

Write the first draft of your essay below. Then, rewrite your final draft on another sheet of paper or on a computer. Read your essay to another person. Does the person agree or disagree with your opinion?

_____

_____

_____

_____

_____

_____

_____

_____

_____

_____

_____

_____

_____

After you score each student's skill assessment pages, match incorrectly answered problems to the table below. Use the corresponding practice pages for any problem areas and ensure that the student receives remediation in these areas to strengthen specific skills.

Answer Key: 1. Answers will vary, but possible answers should relate to the fact that he was alone. 2. C; 3. They are both kind and helpful. Jeremy is young and strong; his grandmother is old and weak. 4. milk and cookies; 5. C; 6. Answers will vary, but possible answers include the use of the personal pronoun *I*, more information about Jeremy's thoughts, and insights into his actions. 7. B; 8. A; 9. D; 10. Yes. The facts may vary but should come from the text. 11. B; 12. B; 13. Answers will vary, but possible answers include the Egyptians needed a good way to communicate and preserve their thoughts and ideas. Papyrus was available, growing on the banks of the Nile. Paper was easier to use for writing than clay or stone tablets. 14. Answers will vary, but possible answers include the Internet, encyclopedias, or books. 15. Answers will vary. 16. Chris **had hoped** to see his favorite athlete in person since the day he **saw** him on TV. 17. <u>Neither</u> the father <u>nor</u> his son had ever run a marathon before. 18. Wow, your garden has tomatoes, zucchini, corn, and carrots growing in it, Stephen. 19. I wrote a story called "My Life as a Chair." 20. Tree frogs sleep during the day and hunt for food at night. 21. mis-in-ter-pret-ed; did not understand correctly; 22. drives me crazy; bothers; 23. The private property belongs to that councilman over there. 24. B; 25. Answers will vary. 26. Answers will vary but should include an introduction, reasons supported by facts, words that link ideas, and a conclusion.

Common Core State Standard*		Test Item(s)	Practice Page(s)
Reading Standards for Literature			
Key Ideas and Details	5.RL.1–5.RL.3	1, 2, 3	13, 17, 19, 21, 25, 27
Craft and Structure	5.RL.4–5.RL.6	4, 5, 6, 7, 8	18, 19, 20, 21
Integration of Knowledge and Ideas	5.RL.7	1, 2, 3	17
Range of Reading and Level of Text Complexity	5.RL.10	Reading passage	14, 16, 18, 20, 22, 23, 24, 26, 48, 49, 50, 51
Reading Standards for Informational Text			
Key Ideas and Details	5.RI.1–5.RI.3	9, 10, 11	28, 29, 31, 33, 37
Craft and Structure	5.RI.4–5.RI.6	12	39, 41, 45
Integration of Knowledge and Ideas	5.RI.7–5.RI.9	13, 14	35, 43, 47
Range of Reading and Level of Text Complexity	5.RI.10	Reading passage	28, 29, 30, 32, 34, 36, 38, 40, 42, 44, 46
Reading Standards: Foundational Skills			
Phonics and Word Recognition	5.RF.3	7, 8	55, 56, 57
Fluency	5.RF.4	1–8	48, 49, 50, 51, 52, 53, 54, 56, 57, 58
Writing Standards			
Text Types and Purposes	5.W.1–5.W.3	24, 26	60, 61, 62, 63, 64, 65, 67, 69, 70, 72, 74
Production and Distribution of Writing	5.W.4–5.W.6	24, 26	59, 68, 71, 75
Language Standards			
Conventions of Standard English	5.L.1–5.L.2	15, 16, 17, 18, 19, 20, 23	76, 77, 78, 79, 80, 81, 82, 83, 84, 85
Knowledge of Language	5.L.3	20, 25	15, 86, 89
Vocabulary Acquisition and Use	5.L.4–5.L.6	21, 22	25, 29, 35, 39, 51, 55, 58, 87, 88, 90

Circle the two words or phrases that are being compared in each sentence. Then, write a sentence to explain the comparison.

1. The row of trees looked like soldiers standing at attention.

_____

2. Looking down from the airplane, the cars were ants crawling along the highway.

_____

3. Twenty circus clowns packed into one little car as sardines are packed in a can.

_____

4. The shadows were ghosts dancing on the sunlit lawn.

_____

5. The sound of waves lapping the shore reminded me of a dog getting a long drink.

_____

6. The baseball flew like a rocket out of the ballpark.

_____

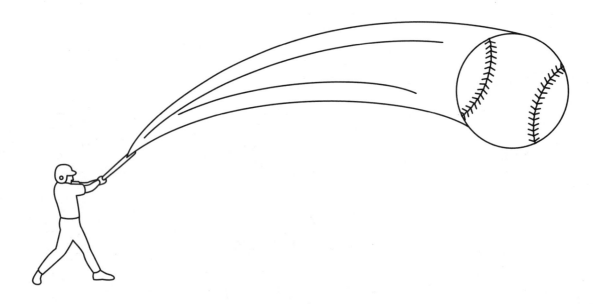

☐ I can determine the meaning of figurative language.

Read the story. Then, circle the phrase that best completes each sentence. Write a quote from the text that supports the answer.

Family Vacation

Before the Atkins family began to pack for their vacation, they made a list of what they would need. Then, they laid out the needed clothes on the dining room table. They each had three pairs of shorts, three T-shirts, a swimsuit, socks, and shoes. They placed their tents, sleeping bags, raincoats, flashlights, bug spray, cooking equipment, and fishing gear on the dining room floor.

They packed the camping equipment and a duffel bag filled with their clothes in the car. They were off! In a couple of hours, they got to the campsite. After setting up camp, they headed for a swim. They ran shoeless to the water and jumped in. After swimming, they had to shower because they were muddy. They hung their suits on trees to dry. While Mom prepared dinner at the campsite, Dad and the children went back to the lake with their poles and bait.

1. The Atkins's family vacation was _____.   by the seashore   by a lake

_____

2. They planned to be away _____.   for a long weekend   for two weeks

_____

3. They were hoping to _____.   eat at restaurants   eat fish they caught

_____

4. They swam in a _____.   lake   swimming pool

_____

☐ **I can use direct evidence from a text to explain and draw inferences.**

Read the poem.

Eldorado

by Edgar Allan Poe

Gaily bedight,
A gallant knight,
In sunshine and in shadow,
Had journeyed long,
Singing a song,
In search of Eldorado.

But he grew old—
This knight so bold—
And o'er his heart a shadow
Fell as he found
No spot of ground
That looked like Eldorado.

And, as his strength
Failed him at length,
He met a pilgrim shadow—
"Shadow," said he,
"Where can it be—
This land of Eldorado?"

"Over the Mountains
Of the Moon,
Down the Valley of the Shadow,
Ride, boldly ride,"
The shade replied,—
"If you seek for Eldorado!"

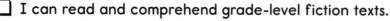

☐ **I can read and comprehend grade-level fiction texts.**

After reading the poem "Eldorado" (page 14), answer the questions.

1. The phrase "gaily bedight, a gallant knight" reflects the language of the time the poem was written. Circle the phrase that best restates the phrase in the language of a fifth grader today. Use a dictionary if needed.

    A. a happy, sleepy, nobleman

    B. a bright, sleepy soldier

    C. brightly dressed, a brave soldier

    D. happily dressed, a nobleman

2. Explain how the author uses repetition in each stanza.

_____

_____

3. Why does the author divide the poem into stanzas?

_____

_____

4. What happens to the knight in the poem? Quote a phrase to support your answer.

_____

_____

5. El Dorado is a legendary golden city that is filled with treasure and precious jewels. Many explorers have searched for the city, but it has never been found. Knowing this, what do you think Poe's message is in "Eldorado"?

_____

_____

☐ **I can explain the importance of chapters, scenes, or stanzas in a text.**
☐ **I can compare and contrast varieties of English in written works.**

Read the story.

The Hero of Harlem
by Sara Cone Bryant (adapted)

Long ago, a boy named Hans lived in a small town in Holland called Harlem. One day, Hans took his little brother out to play to the edge of the town near the dike. As the boys were playing, the little brother commented, "Look, Hans, the dike has a hole."

Hans looked at the hole in the dike and saw a drop of water bubbling slowly through the hole. He knew that all the water needed was a little hole, and soon, it would burst through the dike, flooding the whole town. Almost without thinking, Hans stuck his finger into the hole and told his little brother to run to town and warn the townspeople that there was a hole in the dike.

For a long time, Hans knelt with his finger in the hole in the dike. His hand began to feel numb, and the cold began to creep up his arm. It seemed as if hours had gone by since his brother left. He stared down the road, straining to see someone, but there was no one.

As his ear touched the dike, he thought he heard the voice of the ocean murmuring, "I am the great sea. No one can stand against me. You are only a little boy. Do you think that you can keep me out?"

Hans instinctively started to pull his finger from the dike to run before the sea broke through, and it was too late to escape. He thought of the sea bursting through the dike and imagined a great flood spreading far over the land, leaving ruin in its wake. As he thought of this, he gritted his teeth and shoved his finger into the dike tighter than before.

At that moment, he heard a shout. In the distance, he saw the townspeople dashing down the road carrying pickaxes and shovels. "Hold on! We're coming!" they shouted.

It seemed like only a moment before the crowd was there. When they saw Hans with his finger wedged tightly into the hole in the dike, they gave a robust cheer. When the dike was fixed, they hoisted him onto their shoulders and carried him to town as a hero. To this day, people still tell the story of Hans, the boy who saved Harlem.

☐ **I can read and comprehend grade-level fiction texts.**

After reading "The Hero of Harlem" (page 16), answer the questions.

1. Summarize the story in one sentence. Your summary should include the main characters, the conflict, and the resolution.

_____

_____

2. Using the image and the text, tell what a *dike* is.

_____

_____

3. Without the image, would you have known what a *dike* is? Explain.

_____

_____

4. Circle the sentence that best describes the theme of the story.
   A. Water can be a destructive force.
   B. Never give up. No one is too small to make a difference.
   C. Being a hero is an important goal.
   D. Brothers should stick together.

5. *Personification* is a literary technique used to give human qualities to a nonliving thing. Write an example of personification used in this story.

_____

_____

☐ I can use specific details to summarize the text and determine the theme.
☐ I can analyze graphics or images and determine what they add to a text.

Read the story.

The Burning of the Rice Fields
by Sara Cone Bryant (adapted)

An old man lived on a mountaintop in Japan. At the base of the mountain was a small village. On one side of this village was the mountain, and on the other side was the sea. There was no room for planting crops at the base of the mountain. The land around the old man's house on the mountaintop, however, was flat and fertile. Because of this, the people who lived in the village planted their rice fields around his house. The old man enjoyed looking down the mountain at the village below, out at the blue sea that spanned the horizon, and over the rice fields growing plentiful around his small house. The old man loved the rice fields. He knew that the fields provided food for all of the villagers.

One day, the old man was passing time looking out at the sea. Suddenly, he saw something strange far off where the sea meets the sky. Something like a great cloud was rising, as if the sea was lifting itself into the sky. The old man grabbed a brand from the hearth and ran to the rice fields, where he thrust the burning brand into the ripe, dry rice. The flames ran up the dry stalks, and the entire field was ablaze in an instant. Thick, black smoke billowed into the sky. The villagers below saw the smoke and knew that their rice fields were on fire. Men, women, and children climbed the mountain as fast as they could to save the rice. No one stayed behind.

When they came to the mountaintop and saw the flaming fields of rice, they cried, "Who has done this? How did this happen?"

"I set the fire," said the old man solemnly.

The villagers gathered fiercely around the old man and demanded to know why he had burned their fields. The old man turned and pointed to the sea. The calm blue sea had been replaced by a mighty wall of water that was rolling toward the land. The villagers fell silent at the terrible sight. As they watched, the wall of water rolled over the land, passed over the place where the village had been, and broke with an awful crash against the mountainside. Water covered all of the land at the base of the mountain, and the village was destroyed. But, all of the people were safe. When they realized that the old man had saved them from the tsunami, they praised and honored him for his quick thinking and bravery.

☐ I can read and comprehend grade-level fiction texts.

After reading "The Hero of Harlem" (page 16) and "The Burning of the Rice Fields" (page 18), answer the questions.

1. Summarize "The Burning of the Rice Fields" in one sentence. Your summary should include the main characters, the conflict, and the resolution.

   _____

   _____

2. Complete the Venn diagram to show the similarities and differences between the characters, settings, and events of "The Hero of Harlem" and "The Burning of the Rice Fields."

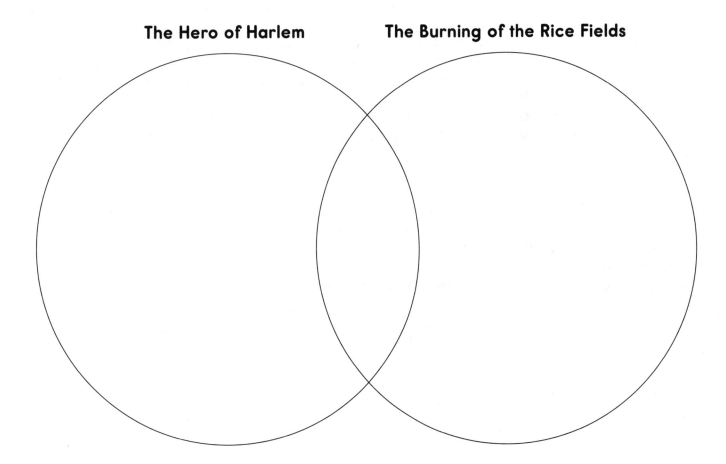

The Hero of Harlem   **The Burning of the Rice Fields**

☐ I can use specific details to summarize the text.
☐ I can use specific details from a text to compare and contrast characters, settings, or events.

Read the story.

The Yew Tree
by Ruedigar Matthes (adapted)

Long ago in Scotland, Finlay, a 12-year-old boy with messy red hair, was walking along the river's edge. Finlay was a good boy with a good heart, but he had had a hard life and little good fortune. As an orphan, Finlay had lived with many different uncles and aunts, none of whom had really welcomed him, and he never stayed long in one place. But, Finlay's misfortune was about to change.

As Finlay walked by the river's edge on this particular day, he slipped on a mossy rock and fell headlong into the frigid water. He landed with a splash, hitting his head on a rock. Finlay's mind went blank as the swift current carried him away.

Finlay woke to a small lamb licking his face. He pushed away the lamb, sat up, and rubbed his throbbing head. Finlay looked around the small room and tried to figure out where he was, but he had never seen the green, sheep-covered hills that surrounded the cottage he was in.

"Hello, lad," a warm, booming voice said. "You should be careful, for your head has a large bump, as well as a cut. When I found you, you were soaked from head to toe, lying in a pile of mossy wood on the riverbank."

"I don't really remember what happened. Where am I? And, who are you?"

"I am a shepherd called Murchadh. Who are you?"

"I am called Finlay."

"Well, perhaps you would like a nice bowl of mutton stew?"

"I am starving, and so I will accept your offer of stew, good sir." Finlay ate as if he had not eaten for days. When he was finished, he pushed away the bowl.

Murchadh looked outside and began to speak. "It will be dark soon. You should spend the night here. My home is small, but it has served me well for many years."

"Thank you for everything," Finlay said. "But, I must be home before it gets dark. My uncle will be furious if I am late. Thank you again." He stood up and hastily headed out the door.

(to be continued . . .)

☐ **I can read and comprehend grade-level fiction texts.**

After reading "The Yew Tree" (page 20), answer the questions.

1. Describe the characters Finlay and Murchadh. How are they alike? How are they different? Use details from the story to support your answer.

_____

_____

_____

2. Contrast Finlay's home life with Murchadh's home life. Use details from the story to support your answer.

_____

_____

_____

3. Circle the time setting that best describes when this story took place. Use details from the story to support your answer.
   A. present day
   B. about a hundred years ago
   C. thousands of years ago
   D. millions of years ago

_____

_____

4. Cite evidence from the story that supports the idea that "Finlay's misfortune was about to change."

_____

_____

☐ I can use direct evidence from a text to explain and draw inferences.
☐ I can use specific details from a text to compare and contrast characters, settings, or events.

Read the story.

The Yew Tree
by Ruedigar Matthes (adapted)
(continued from page 20)

(continued from page 20)

After leaving Murchadh's house, Finlay followed a small trail that cut through the hillside. The sun lowered slowly behind the horizon like the curtain at the end of a play. Suddenly, a hungry fox came out of nowhere and startled Finlay. Without thinking, Finlay turned and ran toward Murchadh's home with the fox on his heels. As he grew tired of running, Finlay stopped and climbed the closest tree—a dead yew tree. The fox paced around the foot of the tree for a few minutes and then turned and jogged away. Just to be sure that he had escaped the fox, Finlay decided to stay in the tree for a while. Soon, he fell asleep to the soft gurgling of a nearby stream.

While he slept, Finlay dreamed that the yew tree curled around his body and kept him warm. He dreamt of a voice whispering the secret to finding good fortune. When he awoke, Finlay looked around. The world seemed different—the sun shone brightly, and the sky was a brilliant blue. Finlay wanted to stay under that sky forever. He decided that he would go back to Murchadh's house and live with him. He climbed down from the tangled branches of the tree and ran toward Murchadh's house.

On his way, Finlay became thirsty and knelt to drink from the nearby stream. After quenching his thirst, he noticed a strange, bright rock. He plucked it from the stream, placed it in his pocket, and continued walking down the path. When he spotted Murchadh's house, he ran as fast as could and burst breathlessly through the door.

"I want to stay and live with you," Finlay blurted out. "I will be a shepherd, and I will work very hard. I promise." He told Murchadh all about his night in the yew. When Finlay finished his story, Murchadh said, "There is a legend about a man who climbed the branches of a yew tree and never came down. According to the legend, if you climb the yew tree and stay awhile, the man will whisper in your ear the way to go to find good fortune. Maybe the yew tree told you to come help a poor shepherd who is getting too old to tend his sheep."

As Finlay embraced the old man, the rock he had found in the stream earlier fell from his pocket. "I found this unusual rock," he said.

"My goodness, lad, this is gold! The voice in the yew tree did tell you where to find fortune!" For the first time in as long as he could remember, Finlay felt fortunate.

☐ **I can read and comprehend grade-level fiction texts.**

After reading "The Hero of Harlem" (page 16) and "The Yew Tree" (pages 20 and 22), answer the questions, comparing the two stories.

1. Summarize the story "The Yew Tree." Your summary should include the main characters, the conflict, and the resolution.

_____

_____

2. Circle the sentence that best describes the theme of "The Yew Tree."
   A. Good fortune comes to good people.
   B. Trees bring good luck.
   C. Shepherds care for sheep and children.
   D. Good fortune only happens in stories.

3. The stories "The Hero of Harlem" and "The Yew Tree" are both folk tales. Complete the graphic organizer to compare and contrast the two stories.

Folk Tale Characteristics	"The Hero of Harlem"	"The Yew Tree"
Ordinary Characters		
StoryTeller's Beginning		
A Problem to Solve		
A Happy Ending		
A Positive Theme		

☐ **I can compare and contrast themes and topics in stories from the same genre.**

Read the story.

River Climbing

Standing knee-deep in the cold rapids, I watched the river carry leaves, sticks, and a few bird feathers. It felt as if the river wanted to carry me too.

"Let go of the tree branch, Jess," Jim said.

Jim was squatting on a big rock in the middle of the river. Jim was big and strong; he seemed afraid of nothing. He was always trying to convince me that I was as brave as he was. When I was in third grade, Jim told me that I could jump off the roof of our shed and land on my feet, but he was wrong. I ended up with my leg in a cast. Maybe Jim was wrong about river climbing too—that is what Jim called this quest we were on.

Jim was yelling to me, cheering for me like he did when I teetered on top of that old roof. I fought my way upstream against the water to make it to him. But, the water seemed colder than usual, and the river acted hungry, as if it wanted to eat me. I stubbed my toe, but I could not feel it because I was numb from the knees down. I was getting tired, and I guess that Jim could tell because he told me to hurry.

"Come on, Jess, don't be such a slowpoke," he teased.

I glared at Jim, clenched my teeth, and pushed my body through the water toward him. As I stepped, I slipped on a slimy rock and twisted my ankle. Pain shot up my leg as I lost my balance and tumbled into the freezing current. I stopped fighting and let the river take me away.

"Where are you going?" Jim yelled. "Come on; get up and try again!"

I ignored him and floated to the side of the river, where I grabbed another tree branch. I pulled my body out of the water and lay on the riverbank, inviting the sun to warm me. Then, I found an easier way upstream. I limped barefoot through the shallow water across some stones and sticks to where Jim lay on the rocks. My ankle still hurt from twisting it, but I did not show that I was hurting. My wet clothes stuck to my body.

(to be continued . . .)

☐ **I can read and comprehend grade-level fiction texts.**

Name_____

After reading "River Climbing" (page 24), answer the questions.

1. Who is telling the story?_____

2. What evidence from the story supports your answer to question 1?

_____

_____

3. Complete the Venn diagram to compare and contrast Jess and Jim.

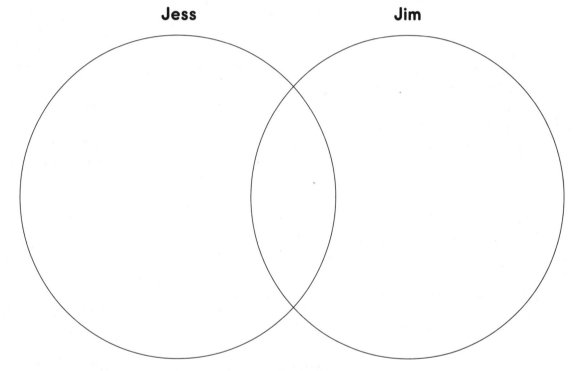

Jess   **Jim**

4. How would the story be different if Jim were telling the story?

_____

_____

5. What are *rapids*? Use clues from the story to help you understand the meaning.

_____

☐ I can use specific details from a text to compare and contrast characters, settings, or events.
☐ I can describe how point of view affects a story.
☐ I can use context clues to understand an unfamiliar word or phrase.

Read the story.

River Climbing
(continued from page 24)

I imagined standing under the sun-warmed waterfall that wound through a craggy rock wall nearby. It was the prize for conquering the river climb.

I did not tell Jim that my ankle hurt from my earlier fall; I thought that he would just tell me to stop being a baby. Instead, I made it to the riverbank and climbed onto the dry rocks. While Jim scrambled ahead, I climbed steadily. Finally, I reached the top, where Jim was yodeling from under the falls.

"You made it!" Jim yelled over the sound of the rushing water. I sat near the falls on a slimy rock to catch my breath. I watched Jim play in the waterfall. He wove back and forth like a snake through the rocks on the wall beside the waterfall. He and the water were dancing, turning, and falling. I wished that I were as brave as he was.

Suddenly, Jim began to slip on the slick rocks. He reached out, trying to balance himself, but there was nothing for him to hold onto. I watched Jim's legs buckle under him, and before I knew it, the rush of water pushed him down the mountain of bulging rocks. I saw the blur of his body under the surging water as he fell down the falls.

Without thinking, I rushed to Jim and asked him if he was all right. He had a cut on his forehead, and his leg was bent at an odd angle. I watched him try to move and then yelp like a hurt puppy. He opened his eyes, closed them, and opened them again.

"Jess, help me," he managed to say, looking at me with frightened eyes.

I helped him get to a dry spot on the grass and tried to make him as comfortable as possible. He looked small, not like the Jim I knew. I did not want to leave him, but I knew that I needed to get help. When I finally made it home, I ran inside and told my parents about Jim. Dad and I headed to where Jim lay by the waterfall.

The next day, I woke up early. As I got out of bed, I felt a sharp pain in my ankle. I got dressed quickly, went to Jim's room, and limped fearfully to the side of his bed. Sitting on the edge of his bed, I touched the cast on Jim's broken leg. Jim groaned as he moved his body a little. Then, he opened his eyes.

"Hey, Jess," he said. "Thanks for your help yesterday. You are one brave girl."

☐ **I can read and comprehend grade-level fiction texts.**

After reading "River Climbing" (pages 24 and 26), answer the questions.

1. How did the roles reverse for Jim and Jess in this part of the story?

   _____

   _____

2. Were you surprised that Jess is a girl? Explain.

   _____

   _____

3. Would it have changed what you thought about Jess if you knew she was a girl from the beginning of the story? Explain.

   _____

   _____

4. How would the story have been different if Jim was telling it?

   _____

   _____

5. How would the story have been different if a third-person narrator was telling it?

   _____

   _____

☐ I can use specific details to summarize the text and determine the theme.
☐ I can describe how the point of view affects a story.

Read the passage. Then, answer the questions.

Laws to Live By

Laws are rules that we live by every day. Imagine if drivers paid no attention to stoplights, if pedestrians crossed roads wherever and whenever they wanted, or if speed limits did not exist. Traffic laws maintain safety and also protect the rights of others.

Laws are enforced by the police and interpreted by the courts. Police officers make sure that the laws are obeyed, and courts enforce the laws. Judges in the courts make sure that laws are carried out fairly and "according to the law."

Courts in the United States have three responsibilities. First, they interpret the laws and make sure that they are followed by everyone. Second, the courts determine punishment for those who are found guilty of breaking the laws. Finally, they must protect the rights of every individual.

Laws can be changed to meet the needs of a nation. Although laws have changed over the years, the principles that govern the judicial system have not. These principles ensure that everyone is protected equally under the law and has a right to a fair trial with a fitting punishment for a crime. But, most important, these principles guarantee that every citizen has the right to practice the many freedoms specified in the US Constitution.

1. What is the main idea of the passage?

_____

_____

2. List three ideas that support the main idea.

_____

_____

_____

3. Why do we have laws?

_____

_____

☐ I can summarize a text by determining the main idea and details of the text.
☐ I can read and comprehend grade-level informational texts.

Name_____

Read the passage.

Highest Court in the Land

The US Supreme Court is the highest court in the United States. It considers thousands of cases each year, but usually, fewer than 200 cases actually are heard before the Supreme Court. The cases that the Supreme Court hears either are of national importance or challenge a law based on constitutional grounds.

Every case that comes before the Supreme Court is given the name of the parties involved. If Mr. Jones is suing the US government, the case is called Jones v. the United States. When the justices decide a case, it becomes a precedent, which means that the decision becomes the basis for future rulings.

All Supreme Court justices are appointed by the president and approved by the Senate. Supreme Court justices may hold their seats until they die. However, if a justice acts improperly or shows corruptness, the justice may be impeached and removed from the Court.

The Supreme Court's most important duty is to maintain the laws as they are presented in the US Constitution. The authors of the Constitution could not have known what life would be like in the twenty-first century. Therefore, it is up to the Supreme Court to interpret the Constitution as it relates to current practices.

Read each statement. Circle *T* if the statement is true. Circle *F* if the statement is false.

1. A case regarding a speeding ticket would be heard by the Supreme Court.   T   F

2. Supreme Court justices are above the law.   T   F

3. Supreme Court justices study the US Constitution.   T   F

4. The word *precedent* means an authoritative example.   T   F

5. The word *impeached* means to remove a law from the Constitution.   T   F

☐ **I can use direct evidence from a text to explain and draw inferences.**
☐ **I can read and comprehend grade-level informational texts.**
☐ **I can use context clues to understand an unfamiliar word or phrase.**

Read the story.

Maria Sklodowska

Have you heard of Maria Sklodowska? Probably not. But, you may have heard of Marie Curie. This is a real-life story of how a poor, young Polish girl grew up to become a world-famous scientist.

Maria Sklodowska was born on November 7, 1867, in Warsaw, Poland. She grew up in an area of Poland where learning was considered a privilege. Her father was a professor. Although she grew up without much money, she was surrounded by science equipment. In 1891, she went to Paris, France, to go to college. While in France, she began to use the French spelling of her first name Marie.

Sklodowska received her physics degree in 1893, graduating first in her class. In 1894, she earned a mathematics degree, graduating second in her class. She met a scientist named Pierre Curie. They were married in 1895. The husband-and-wife team became known worldwide for their work. They studied radioactivity. The Curies made many new discoveries. Marie Curie was awarded the Nobel Prize. She later became the first female professor at the university in Paris.

She died on July 4, 1934, of a disease caused by her work with radioactive materials.

☐ I can read and comprehend grade-level informational texts.

After reading "Maria Sklodowska" (page 30), follow the directions.

1. Is the passage fiction or nonfiction? Write evidence from the text that supports your answer.

_____

_____

2. Write two accomplishments of Maria Sklodowska that provide evidence that she became a world-famous scientist.

_____

_____

3. Circle the statement you can infer from "learning was considered a privilege."
   A. Everyone went to school.
   B. Only the rich went to school.
4. Create a time line of Maria Sklodowska's life.

☐ **I can use direct evidence from a text to explain and draw inferences.**

5.RI.10

Read the passage.

Louis Pasteur

Louis Pasteur was a famous scientist. He was born in France in 1822. Pasteur earned a degree as a doctor of science, but he was not a physician. Because he was not a medical doctor, many members of the medical profession did not take his work seriously. Pasteur, however, believed strongly that germs existed and that they caused disease. He discovered a way to control the spread of a silkworm disease. He also developed vaccines for rabies and anthrax. Pasteur made great strides in the medical field.

Pasteur also developed a process to keep milk free of germs. The process involves heating the milk to 140°F (60°C) for 30 minutes. The milk is then cooled quickly and sealed in sterile containers. This process is called pasteurization. Each time you drink a glass of cold milk, you have Pasteur to thank.

In his later years, the medical community recognized the importance of Pasteur's work. In 1888, Pasteur opened a research center in Paris, France. It is called the Pasteur Institute. Pasteur directed the work that was done there until his death in 1895. Today, more than 100 years later, scientists at the institute continue to build on his ideas.

☐ I can read and comprehend grade-level informational texts.

After reading "Maria Sklodowska" (page 30) and "Louis Pasteur" (page 32), follow the directions.

1. What evidence from the passage supports the statement, "Louis Pasteur was a famous scientist"?

_____

_____

_____

2. What is a *physician*? _____

3. What does it mean that "Pasteur earned a degree as a doctor of science, but he was not a physician"?

_____

_____

4. Do you think that Louis Pasteur and Maria Sklodowska knew of each other's work? Use evidence from the passages to support your answer.

_____

_____

5. Draw a time line of Louis Pasteur's life. Add the dates of Maria Sklodowska's birth and death to the time line.

☐ I can explain how people, events, ideas, or concepts are connected in a historical, scientific, or technical text.

Read the passage.

Underwater Cities

A coral reef is an underwater delight. A coral reef is like a busy city. The surprising builders of these "cities" are little animals called polyps. Polyps are usually no bigger than peas. They look like tiny flowers creating a colorful garden.

The coral polyps take in calcium from the seawater. They change the calcium into limestone. They use the limestone to form skeletons to support their soft bodies. The coral polyps live in colonies, with each polyp attached to its neighbor. As the polyps grow, they build new skeletons on top of the old ones. The formations built by millions of polyps are called coral reefs. The structures formed by the polyps may be branches, cups, ripples, discs, fans, or columns. Each kind of coral grows in a pattern.

Coral reefs provide a habitat for many other animals. The reefs can be home to moray eels, soft corals, sponges, tube worms, barracudas, sharks, starfish, manta rays, sea turtles, lobsters, crabs, shrimp, and colorful fish.

Coral fossils show that coral reefs have existed in the sea for millions of years. The solid appearance of reefs makes them seem sturdy. Actually, coral reefs are fragile. A change in the temperature, the quality of the water, or the amount of light can kill the coral polyps.

Some destruction of coral reefs is from natural causes, but people cause the greatest damage to reefs. Once a reef is damaged, it may never recover. When that happens, the entire coral community is lost. It is important that people take care of these beautiful underwater cities.

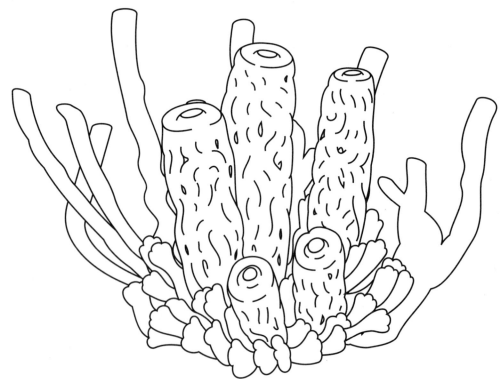

☐ I can read and comprehend grade-level informational texts.

© Carson-Dellosa • CD-104612

After reading "Underwater Cities" (page 34), follow the directions.

1. How does the author feel about coral reefs? Use evidence from the passage to support your answer.

_____

_____

_____

2. What human activities do you think cause damage to coral reefs?

_____

_____

_____

3. List two similes the author uses to describe coral reefs.

_____

_____

4. Use details from the passage and prior knowledge you may have about coral reefs to draw a picture of a coral reef.

☐ I can find evidence from the text to support what the author believes or wants me to believe about a certain topic.
☐ I can interpret figurative language in a text.

Read the passage.

The Truth about History

History is not always what it seems. Imagine that your favorite basketball team is the Houston Rockets. You missed an unbelievable game they played against the Los Angeles Lakers. You know that the Rockets won, but you want to find out how they won. When you ask your friends about the game, they each tell you something different.

For example, during overtime, the referees called a controversial foul. One of your friends says, "The Lakers would have won the game if it weren't for that call." Another friend argues that the foul was a good call. Both sides mix facts with their opinions about what they saw.

You decide to check the newspapers for the real story. At the library, you look at newspapers from both Houston, Texas, and Los Angeles, California. The stories from these two newspapers disagree. Both sides sound good, but both sides cannot tell the whole truth.

Next, you decide to watch a video of the game. Even the instant replay is not very clear.

It is difficult to get to the truth about something that you did not witness. Imagine a game that was played 100 years ago. You would have to rely on written accounts, such as newspaper articles from that time or a diary kept by one of the players. Historians look at evidence like this to help recreate historic events. But, many of these events are much more complicated than the outcome of a basketball game. Think about how many different opinions there are about the American Revolution.

History can be defined as a "best guess." When we try to look at history, it is almost as if we are detectives trying to piece together clues. We have to decide what happened based on the evidence left behind. We cannot know for sure because we were not there.

☐ I can read and comprehend grade-level informational texts.

After reading "The Truth about History" (page 36), answer the questions.

1. What is the main idea of the passage?

_____

_____

2. List three details from the passage that support the main idea.

_____

_____

_____

3. How is history similar to learning about a basketball game that you did not attend?

_____

_____

4. The passage mentions reading newspaper articles and diaries as ways of learning about the past. What are some other ways to learn about history?

_____

_____

5. Do you agree with the author's idea of what history is? Explain.

_____

_____

_____

☐ **I can summarize a text by determining the main ideas and details of the text.**

Read the passage.

Immigration at Angel Island

In 1882, Congress passed a law called the Chinese Exclusion Act. It was passed to keep Chinese people from *immigrating* to America. Chinese workers had come to the United States to work as *merchants* or in mines. They helped build railroads. But, some Americans were afraid that Chinese people would take their jobs. The law made it hard for Chinese people to enter the country. It said that only the relatives of citizens would be allowed in. No other people faced such *discrimination*.

At that time, there was a large section of San Francisco, California, called Chinatown. Thousands of Chinese people went there. In 1906, San Francisco had a large earthquake. A fire started because of the earthquake. The fire destroyed much of the city. When Chinatown burned, so did many records of *citizenship*. The government did not know which Chinese people coming to America were related to citizens. The people who were related to citizens would be able to stay. The other people would have to return to China.

In 1910, the government opened a station for immigrants. The station was built on Angel Island in San Francisco's *harbor*. Each Chinese immigrant had to wait there until he could prove that he had a relative who was a citizen. The average Chinese immigrant was *detained* on the island for two to three weeks. However, some people spent months or even years at the Immigration Station. Some Chinese immigrants told stories of their experiences through poetry that they carved on the walls of the wooden *barracks* where they lived.

The Chinese Exclusion Act was *repealed* in 1943. More than 250,000 Chinese immigrants came through Angel Island. Today, it is a state park with bike trails, hiking trails, camping spots, and boats. The barracks where immigrants lived are a historic site. The poetry they carved there has been translated into English.

☐ **I can read and comprehend grade-level informational texts.**

Name_____

After reading "Immigration at Angel Island" (page 38), answer the questions.

1. What is the main idea of the passage?

_____

_____

Match each word with its definition.

2. _____ unfair treatment of a group of people   A. barracks

3. _____ people who buy and sell goods   B. detained

4. _____ a place along the ocean where ships dock   C. discrimination

5. _____ membership in a country   D. immigrating

6. _____ canceled or withdrawn   E. harbor

7. _____ coming to a country from another one   F. citizenship

8. _____ temporary buildings that house many people   G. merchants

9. _____ held   H. repealed

☐ I can determine the meaning of words and phrases in an informational text.
☐ I can use context clues to understand an unfamiliar word or phrase.

Read the play.

Poems from Angel Island

Tour Guide: Welcome to the Angel Island Immigration Station. Surrounding you in these barracks are records of the people who stayed here from 1910 to 1940. What do you see on this wall?

Student 1: Writing has been carved into the wood, and it is in another language.

Tour Guide: The language is Chinese. Our translators, Lin and Hai, will help us read what it says.

Lin: This part says, "I took a raft and sailed the seas. Rising early at dawn with the stars above my head. Traveling deep into the night, the moon my companion."

Hai: "Who knew my trip would be full of rain and snow?"

Tour Guide: Many Chinese people left their homes and sailed to America. When they got here, they had to wait to become citizens. They were detained in these small wooden barracks.

Student 2: Why did they write on the walls?

Tour Guide: Imagine you were forced to live in a place such as this. How would you feel?

Student 2: I would feel angry or maybe sad.

Tour Guide: Other poems carved into the walls tell us more about how the Chinese people felt.

Lin: Here, it says, "I have walked to the very edge of the earth. A dusty, windy journey. I am worn out. Who can save me? I am like a fish out of water."

Hai: "I worry for my parents, my wife, and my son. Do they have enough firewood and food?"

Lin: "We are kept in a dark, filthy room. Who would have thought that my joy would turn into sorrow?"

Hai: "Cruel treatment, not one breath of fresh air. Little food, many restrictions. Here, even a proud man bows his head low."

Tour Guide: Thanks, Lin and Hai, for translating today. We can learn from mistakes by studying history. The words carved into this wall are preserved so that we remember the past and learn from it.

☐ **I can read and comprehend grade-level informational texts.**

After reading *Immigration at Angel Island* (page 38) and *Poems from Angel Island* (page 40), answer the questions.

1. What is the topic of both "Immigration at Angel Island" and *Poems from Angel Island?*

_____

_____

2. What is the purpose of both "Immigration at Angel Island" and *Poems from Angel Island?*

_____

_____

3. What information is provided in both "Immigration at Angel Island" and *Poems from Angel Island?*

_____

_____

4. What information is provided in "Immigration at Angel Island" but not in *Poems from Angel Island?*

_____

_____

5. What information is provided in *Poems from Angel Island* but not in "Immigration at Angel Island"?

_____

_____

❑ **I can identify, compare, and contrast different accounts of the same event of topic.**

Read the passage.

A Pioneer of Flight

A Budding Interest

Amelia Earhart saw an airplane for the first time at a state fair in 1907. She was 10 years old. Not until a decade later, while attending a stunt-flying exhibition, did she really become interested in flying.

A Rise to Fame

As a social worker, Earhart had never had any experience with airplanes. Determined to learn how to fly, she took her first lesson in 1921. In just six months, she saved enough money to buy her own airplane. It was bright yellow. She named it Canary. She set her first record in it. She became the first woman to fly up to 14,000 feet (4267 m).

Earhart flew often. Her hard work paid off in 1928 when a book publisher named George P. Putnam asked her if she would fly across the Atlantic Ocean. Her answer was yes. She became a celebrity. From that point on, Earhart's life centered on flying. She became popular as she won competitions and awards.

Earhart married George Putnam in 1931. Together, they planned her solo trek across the Atlantic Ocean in 1932. When she returned home, President Herbert Hoover awarded her a medal. More medals followed. In 1935, she became the first person to fly solo from Hawaii to California.

A Mysterious End

Earhart set a new goal. She wanted to be the first woman to fly around the world. Despite a failed first attempt, Earhart departed from Florida in 1937. Navigator Fred Noonan flew with her. During this flight, they disappeared. Earhart tried to land on a small island in the Pacific Ocean. She missed the island because of cloudy conditions. Her airplane never landed. A rescue attempt began immediately. They never found Earhart or her airplane, but she lives on as a legend in aviation history.

☐ **I can read and comprehend grade-level informational texts.**

After reading "A Pioneer of Flight" (page 42), follow the directions.

1. Make a time line of the events that led Amelia Earhart to become an aviator.

2. Write a newspaper article that reports Amelia Earhart's disappearance. Use the five W's: who, what, when, why, and where.

_____

_____

_____

_____

_____

3. Since 1937, people have searched unsuccessfully for Amelia Earhart's airplane. There are many theories about what happened. What do you think happened to Amelia Earhart? Use evidence from the text to support your thinking.

_____

_____

_____

☐ I can quickly find evidence in the text to support my thinking when answering a question or solving a problem.

Read the passage.

John Colter: Western Explorer

A Wilderness Traveler

John Colter explored more of the American wilderness than nearly any explorer of his time. He was one of the first settlers to cross North America and see the Pacific Ocean. He traveled through the American Indian territories. He saw amazing natural wonders.

Exploring

In 1804, Colter set off into the unknown wilderness of the American West. He traveled with a group called the Corps of Discovery. Lewis and Clark led the group. The Corps included 32 men, a young American Indian woman named Sacagawea, and her baby. The goal was to find a waterway that connected the Missouri River and the Pacific Ocean. The corps members suffered hardship, hunger, sickness, and fatigue.

Fur Trapping

After nearly two years in the wilderness, the Corps of Discovery was headed back to St. Louis, Missouri. They met a company of fur trappers coming up the Missouri River. The company was eager to gain information about the wilderness, so Colter decided to join them and be their guide. On one of his trips, Colter came across a strange landscape. Water boiled from the earth and shot 70 feet (21 m) into the air. Thick mud bubbled from stinking pools and filled the air with a foul stench. All kinds of wild animals roamed freely through this land of beauty. Today, we call the area Yellowstone National Park.

John Colter lived a life of adventure. But, how did he die? No one knows for sure, but many historians believe that his death was neither violent nor heroic. According to some accounts, Colter died at home in his bed.

☐ I can read and comprehend grade-level informational texts.

After reading "A Pioneer of Flight" (page 42) and "John Colter: Western Explorer" (page 44), answer the questions.

1. What is John Colter famous for? Use evidence from the passage to support your answer.

_____

_____

_____

2. What are some similarities between John Colter and Amelia Earhart?

_____

_____

_____

3. Compare the organization of "A Pioneer of Flight" and "John Colter: Western Explorer." How are they alike?

_____

_____

_____

4. Contrast the organization of "A Pioneer of Flight" and "John Colter: Western Explorer." How are they different?

_____

_____

_____

❑ **I can compare and contrast the organizational structures of different texts.**

Read the passage.

John Colter's Escape

John Colter became a legend of the great expansion. One story is told about how he escaped from a tribe of American Indians. Members of the Blackfoot tribe captured him and his traveling companion, John Potts. Potts was shot, and Colter was taken back to their camp. They took his clothes and his shoes. They held a council to decide his fate. Colter could understand some of their language, and he heard them discussing how to do away with him.

The chief told Colter to start walking away from the camp. After he had walked a few hundred yards, someone yelled. All of the braves in the camp sprinted after him. The Yellowstone River was five miles away. Colter knew that if he could get to the river, he might have a chance of escaping the tribe. The ground was rough and covered with sharp rocks and prickly pear cacti. The braves wore thick moccasins. Colter raced for his life on bare feet. The soles of his feet were soon covered with cactus needles. Several braves were gaining on him. He could have given up, but his will to live roared like a great fire within him. He pushed himself to run faster.

He called upon every bit of strength and energy he had in his body. After a couple of miles, his nose started to bleed. At last, he reached the river and dove in. The icy water washed away the blood and soothed his torn feet. He hid in the river as the braves searched for him. He stayed in the river until dark. Then, he crawled out to finish his escape. He climbed a mountain in the dark and finally stumbled into a trading post a few weeks later.

Although John Colter blazed trails with Lewis and Clark, explored a vast wilderness, and discovered fabulous geysers, his greatest discovery was learning how strong his will to live could be.

I can read and comprehend grade-level informational texts.

After reading "John Colter: Western Explorer" (page 44) and "John Colter's Escape" (page 46), use the graphic organizer to plan information for a brief report about John Colter. Then, write a report on another sheet of paper or on a computer.

Title:
Introductory Sentence Stating Main Idea:
Supporting Detail or Fact from the Passages:
Supporting Detail or Fact from the Passages:
Supporting Detail or Fact from the Passages:
Concluding Sentence Summarizing the Main Idea:

☐ **I can use information from different texts to write or talk about subjects.**

Read the fable aloud to another person. Then, follow the directions.

The Hare and the Tortoise

One day, an arrogant hare teased a humble tortoise.

"You are so slow that I can walk backward and keep up with you," taunted the hare.

So, the tortoise challenged the hare to a race. The hare, of course, was so confident that he would win that when he got far ahead enough, he stopped for a rest and soon fell asleep. The tortoise, on the other hand, continued plodding along at his slow pace, never stopping. When the hare woke up, he realized he had slept much longer than he intended. He ran as fast as he could to the finish line. He arrived just in time to see the tortoise crossing the finish line before him.

1. Have the person that you read the fable to sign here: _____

2. With what emphasis or emotion did you read the sentence, "You are so slow that I can walk backward and keep up with you"?

_____

3. *Arrogant* and *humble* are antonyms. Use clues from the fable to help you define the words. Write the definitions.

   A. arrogant: _____

   B. humble: _____

4. Write the word from the fable that is a synonym for the word *teased*.

_____

5. Finish the analogy: Hare is to rabbit as tortoise is to _____.

☐ I can read aloud with accuracy, fluency, and expression.
☐ I can uses context clues and reread the text to understand unfamiliar words.
☐ I can read and comprehend grade-level fiction texts.

Read the fable aloud to another person. Think about the moral or lesson that the fable describes. Then, follow the directions.

The Fox and the Crow

A crow sat in a tree with a piece of cheese that he had just taken from an open window. A red fox, who walking by, saw the crow and wanted the cheese. The red fox had a plan to get the cheese from the bird.

"My dear friend," the fox said sweetly to the crow, "I hear that you sing a beautiful song. Would you be so kind as to sing for me?"

The crow indeed felt proud. To prove his voice, the crow opened his mouth to sing. As his mouth opened, the cheese fell out, and the crafty red fox gobbled it up.

1. Have the person that you read the fable to sign here: _____

2. With what emphasis did you read the sentence, "My dear friend, I hear that you sing a beautiful song. Would you be so kind as to sing for me"?

_____

3. What is the moral or lesson of this fable?

_____

4. Finish the analogy: Red fox is to fox as crow is to _____.

☐ I can read with purpose and understanding.
☐ I can read aloud with accuracy, fluency, and expression.
☐ I can read and comprehend grade-level fiction texts.

Practice reading the poem aloud. Think about the way the author compares winter to a white owl. Then, read the poem to another person.

Winter Is a White Owl

by Alisha Golden

The owl's eyes shine darkly,
As the quiet moon at midnight.
So chillingly cold,
So dark and black.
The snow falls gently,
Like the downy feathers
Of the night watcher.
He floats from tree to limb,
Ever watchful,
In the frosty winter night.
The moon casts her pale light
On the soft snow.
Nature is in silent slumber,
Deeply buried
Under a blanket of white crystals.
The owl is alone,
Except for the moon.
All is still.

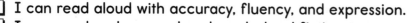

☐ **I can read aloud with accuracy, fluency, and expression.**
☐ **I can read and comprehend grade-level fiction texts.**

After reading aloud "Winter Is a White Owl" (page 50), follow the directions.

1. Have the person you read the poem to sign here. _____

2. What tone did you use when you read this poem aloud? _____

3. Complete the chart with phrases the author uses to describe winter and the white owl.

Descriptions of the White Owl	Descriptions of Winter

4. What simile does the author use to describe snow falling? _____

5. Did you enjoy reading this poem? Why or why not?

_____

_____

☐ I can read with purpose and understanding.
☐ I can interpret figurative language in a text.

Read the poem by Emily Dickinson aloud to another person.

A Bird Came down the Walk—
He did not know I saw—
He bit an angle-worm in halves
And ate the fellow, raw,

And then he drank a Dew
From a convenient Grass,
And then hopped sidewise to the Wall
To let a Beetle pass—

He glanced with rapid eyes
That hurried all abroad—
They looked like frightened Beads, I thought—
He stirred his Velvet Head.

Like one in danger, Cautious,
I offered him a Crumb,
And he unrolled his feathers
And rowed him softer home—

Than Oars divide the Ocean,
Too silver for a seam—
Or Butterflies, off Banks of Noon,
Leap, splashless as they swim.

☐ **I can read aloud with accuracy, fluency, and expression.**

After reading the poem by Emily Dickinson (page 52), answer the questions.

1. Authors write poetry in stanzas for the rhythm and rhyme. Circle the rhyme scheme in this poem.
   A. abcb
   B. abab
   C. abcd
   D. aabb

2. In the poem, Emily Dickinson describes the actions of a bird she is watching. List at least four of the actions she tells about in this poem.

   _____

   _____

3. What did the bird do when he was offered a crumb? _____

   _____

4. What metaphor does the author use to describe the action of the bird when offered a crumb?

   _____

   _____

☐ **I can explain the importance of chapters, scenes, and stanzas in a text.**
☐ **I can read with purpose and understanding.**

Read the passage. Then, follow the directions.

Mr. Versatility

What's your forte? Everyone is good at something. Just ask Ashrita Furman from Brooklyn, New York. He is a world record holder. He has broken 14 records in his life, including the record for being the person who holds the most world records. It's no wonder they call him "Mr. Versatility." He broke his first record in 1979 by doing 27,000 jumping jacks. Now, that's talent!

When Furman was young, he was not good at sports. Today, he has quite a flair for playground games. Furman holds the record for playing the most hopscotch games in 24 hours (434 games), completing the most rope jumps in 24 hours (130,000 jumps), and finishing the fastest 10K sack race (1 hour, 25 minutes, and 10 seconds).

Other records he holds include completing the most underwater rope jumps in one hour (738 jumps) and doing the fastest pogo stick ascent of Canada's CN Tower (57 minutes and 51 seconds). Furman even holds the record for the greatest distance walked while balancing a milk bottle on his head (80.96 miles). It took him 23 hours and 35 minutes to finish his walk. Would you like to have Furman's skills, or is there another gift that you would prefer?

1. What is the main idea of the passage?

_____

_____

2. Based on your reading of the text, what does the word *forte* mean?

_____

3. Write four synonyms for the word *forte* found in the passage.

_____   _____

_____   _____

4. Circle the definition of *record* as used in the passage.
   A. a written account
   B. a disc on which sound is recorded
   C. an unbeaten statistic
   D. an official document

□ **I can use context clues and reread the text to read and understand unfamiliar words.**

Read the passage. Then, follow the directions.

Family of Primates

Monkeys and apes belong to a group called primates. (The word *primate* comes from a Latin word meaning "first.") Monkeys and apes are primates because they have complex brains. They are the most intelligent of all animals. Human beings are also classified as primates. Monkeys and apes have large brains like us and use their front limbs as hands. Monkeys, apes, and humans can think and use tools.

The chimpanzee is the most human looking of the primates. Although chimpanzees eat mostly fruits, they will eat some vegetables. They have even been seen eating insects and killing and eating small animals. Chimpanzees use sticks as tools to get honey from honeycombs or to dig ants and termites from their nests.

1. What is the main idea of the passage? _____

2. Write three facts that support the main idea.

_____

_____

_____

3. The word part *prim* means *first*. Write three other words that contain this word part. Then, write each word's definition. Use a dictionary if needed.

_____

_____

_____

4. Write the word from the passage that is made up of two word parts, *com* meaning "with" and plex meaning "having parts." Then, write a definition for the word.

_____

5. Write the word from the passage that contains the word part hum, meaning "of the earth or mankind." Then, write two other words that have this word part. Use a dictionary if needed.

_____

6. Write the word *chimpanzee* and then divide it into syllables.

_____

☐ I can use my knowledge of letter sounds, syllables, and word parts to read unfamiliar words.
☐ I can use affixes and roots to understand an unfamiliar word or phrase.

5.RF.3a, 5.RF.4c

Read the passage. Then, follow the directions.

The Brain: A Control Panel

The brain is an organ that controls almost everything that the human body does. It is divided into three parts. Each part controls different bodily functions. The three parts are the medulla, the cerebellum, and the cerebrum.

The medulla is located where the spinal cord enters the head. It takes care of involuntary actions. Involuntary actions do not require any decision making. They happen without any thought. Breathing, digestion, and elimination are examples of involuntary actions.

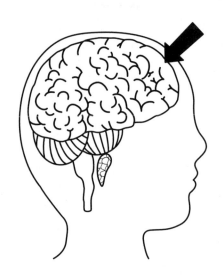

Voluntary movements demand some instruction. Brushing your teeth, dressing, and doing a somersault are examples of voluntary actions. The cerebellum is the part of the brain that controls bodily movements.

The largest part of the brain is the cerebrum. It controls voluntary mental operations, such as speaking, thinking, remembering, learning, and deciding. The cerebrum is divided into two equal parts called hemispheres. The hemispheres are covered by a layer of nerve cells called the cortex. There are many centers located in different areas of the cortex that send and receive messages. Each of the operations that the cerebrum controls is located in a different center.

Divide each word into syllables. Then, use the passage to define each word. Write the meaning on the line.

1. medulla _____

2. cerebellum _____

3. cerebrum _____

4. involuntary _____

5. voluntary _____

☐ **I can use my knowledge of letter sounds, syllables, and word parts to read unfamiliar words.**
☐ **I can use context clues and reread the text to understand unfamiliar words.**

Name_____

Study the words from the passage below. Then, read the passage aloud.

1. *Anasazi* is pronounced \'ä-na-'sä-zē\. Say the word aloud three times. Sign here when you have done so.

_____

2. Divide each of the following words into syllables. Use the word parts to determine the meaning of each word. Write the meaning on the line. Use a dictionary if needed.

   A. prehistoric _____

   B. civilization _____

   C. archaeologist _____

   D. ancestral _____

Now, read the passage aloud to another person.

Ancient People

One prehistoric civilization of the southwestern United States was the Anasazi. No one knows what the Anasazi called themselves. *Anasazi* is the name given to them by archaeologists and scholars who have studied prehistoric American Indians of the Southwest. *Anasazi* is a Navajo word that means "ancient enemy." Over time, the word has come to mean "ancient people."

3. Where might you find a passage like this one?_____

4. Why might you read about the Anasazi? _____

_____

_____

_____

☐ **I can use my knowledge of letter sounds, syllables, and word parts to read and understand unfamiliar words.**
☐ **I can read aloud with accuracy, fluency, and expression.**

Read the passage. Then, write each italicized word next to its definition below.

The Space Age

The space age began in 1957 when the Union of Soviet Socialist Republics (USSR) *launched* the first satellite named *Sputnik 1*. The importance of its mission *transformed* how the world was able to look at space. *Sputnik 1* was the first object to go beyond Earth's *atmosphere*. Since then, thousands of satellites have been launched, mostly by the *former* USSR and the United States.

Satellites are large and heavy. Some weigh several tons. Their *payloads* have a purpose related to the design of each satellite's *mission*. Satellites are designed to perform different tasks, including exploring Earth and space, observing the weather, improving communications, and assisting the military.

Until the space age, there were *theories* about space that could not be proven. They could only be *evaluated* from observations and instruments on the ground. The atmosphere that surrounds Earth *distorts* the way the stars really look because of the substances within the atmosphere. By putting satellites beyond Earth's atmosphere, scientists can get a better picture of distant stars and perhaps the *universe*.

1. the layers of gases surrounding a planet _____

2. released _____

3. tested _____

4. a specific task _____

5. changed _____

6. twists the normal shape _____

7. before in time _____

8. beliefs _____

9. everything in a space system _____

10. loads carried by a satellite necessary for the flight _____

11. the first satellite _____

☐ **I can use context clues and reread the text to understand unfamiliar words.**
☐ **I can learn and use academic and subject specific vocabulary.**

When writing, it is important to consider your audience. Imagine that you are running for class president. Plan a speech telling your classmates why they should vote for you. Answer the questions to help you plan the content of your speech.

1. Who is my audience? _____

2. What is important to my audience?_____

_____

_____

3. What is my audience least likely to care about?_____

_____

_____

4. What do I want my audience to know about me? _____

_____

_____

Write your speech.

_____

_____

_____

_____

_____

_____

_____

_____

_____

☐ **I can consider the purpose and audience when writing.**

Read the paragraph. Write time-order words or phrases on the lines to help the events of the passage flow. You can use the time-order words from the list or write your own. Be sure to include commas as necessary.

at last	at this point	finally	first	in conclusion
in the meantime	meanwhile	next	then	

Growing a Sunflower

Did you know that you can plant a sunflower seed inside a cup? It is simple and fun!

_____ gather the following materials: a clear, plastic cup; a wet paper

towel; and a sunflower seed. _____ place the paper towel inside the cup.

_____ make sure that the paper towel covers the entire inside of the cup. Place

the seed on the paper towel and fold the paper towel over the

seed. _____ place the cup near a window with

a lot of sunlight shining through. If your sunflower does not get

enough sunlight, it will not be able to grow. It will take three weeks

for your seed to sprout. _____ you can record any

changes that you observe. _____ you will be able

to see your sunflower flourish.

❑ **I can use transitional words, phrases, and clauses to help the events in a story flow.**

Many authors create characters based on people they know in real life. Think about someone who is special to you such as a parent, a brother or sister, or a friend. Draw the person's face in the middle of this page. Then, answer the questions.

What does the character look like?

_____

_____

_____

What does the character think?

_____

_____

_____

How does the character act?

_____

_____

_____

What is the character's name?

_____

_____

_____

☐ I can use narrative techniques to enhance the events and the characters in a story.

Use the five senses to describe each setting. Include vivid details in your descriptions.

1. The attic of a house in the winter

_____

_____

_____

_____

2. A lighthouse near the ocean

_____

_____

_____

_____

3. A flower garden in a park

_____

_____

_____

_____

4. A crowded elevator

_____

_____

_____

_____

☐ I can use narrative techniques to enhance the events and the characters in a story.
☐ I can use descriptive words and details to help readers better understand a story.

Use your five senses to help you add details to make your writing more interesting.

1. It was the best cake I've ever had!

The cake looked_____.

The cake smelled_____.

In my mouth, the cake felt _____.

The cake tasted _____.

Use your descriptions to write a few "showing" sentences about the cake.

_____

_____

_____

_____

2. It was a great party.

What did you see at the party?_____

What did you hear at the party? _____

What did you eat at the party?_____

Describe the party using a few "showing" sentences.

_____

_____

_____

_____

☐ I can use narrative techniques to enhance the events and the characters in a story.
☐ I can use descriptive words and details to help readers better understand a story.

Read each story beginning. Then, rewrite the story beginning using descriptive words and details to engage the reader.

1. My family and I are going on a road trip. It will be a great adventure.

_____

_____

_____

2. There is never anything to do on Sunday. Sunday is a very dull day.

_____

_____

_____

3. Baseball is a terrific game. It is very fun.

_____

_____

_____

4. Spaghetti is my favorite food. It is delicious.

_____

_____

_____

❏ I can use descriptive words and details to help readers better understand a story.

Read the story details. Then, write an ending to complete the story.

Character
Ansley is 10 years old. She is hardworking but not athletic.

Problem
Ansley wants to learn how to play soccer.

Solution
She practices with her dad every day until she tries out for the school soccer team.

Satisfying Ending

_____

_____

_____

_____

_____

_____

_____

_____

_____

_____

_____

_____

_____

_____

_____

☐ I can write a conclusion that completes a story.

5.W.9a

To become a better writer, it is important to read. Read "The Hero of Harlem" (page 16). Use the flowchart to help you recognize the strategies the author of this story used.

Setting: _____

Characters: _____

Problem: _____
_____

Event 1: _____
_____
_____
_____
_____
_____
_____

Event 2: _____
_____
_____
_____
_____
_____
_____

Event 3: _____
_____
_____
_____
_____
_____
_____

Solution: _____
_____

☐ I can use grade-level reading strategies when writing about fiction texts.

Write a story. Use the flowchart to help you plan your story.

Setting: _____

Characters: _____

Problem: _____
_____

Event 1: _____

_____
_____
_____
_____
_____
_____

Event 2: _____

_____
_____
_____
_____
_____
_____

Event 3: _____

_____
_____
_____
_____
_____
_____

Solution: _____
_____

☐ **I can establish a situation, introduce characters and a narrator, and organize events in a story.**

Use the editing checklist to produce a final copy of your story (page 67). Type your final draft on a computer or write it on another sheet of paper. Attach your first draft and this editing sheet to your final draft.

Plan

_____ I have made a written plan that outlines the setting, characters, problem, events, and conclusion of my story.

Revise

_____ I have written an interesting start to my story that catches the reader's attention.

_____ I have written a closing that effectively ends my story.

_____ I have revised my writing with vivid and descriptive words.

_____ I used transition words and phrases to connect my writing.

Edit

_____ I used words correctly.

_____ I have written complete sentences.

_____ I have edited my writing for capitalization and punctuation.

_____ I have edited my writing for spelling errors.

Publish

_____ I have decided how I will publish and share my writing.

☐ I can plan, revise, and edit my writing.
☐ I can use technology to create, publish, and show my writing.
☐ I can write over different time frames for various purposes and audiences.

Write an essay to support an opinion you have. Use the graphic organizer to help you state your opinion and organize the reasons that support your opinion.

What is your opinion on the topic?

_____

_____

_____

_____

_____

_____

_____

_____

_____

_____

Whom are you trying to persuade?

_____

_____

_____

_____

_____

_____

_____

_____

_____

_____

List three reasons to support your opinion.

_____

_____

_____

To convince the reader, add supporting facts and details for each reason.

_____

_____

_____

☐ I can organize my writing with a logical progression that supports an opinion.
☐ I can use organized facts and details to support reasons.

Use the following format to organize the first draft of your opinion essay (page 69). Use words and phrases to connect your opinion to your reasons.

also	another	because	consequently	for example
in addition to	since	specifically	such as	therefore

Paragraph 1: State your opinion and the three reasons that support your opinion.

_____

_____

_____

Paragraph 2: State your first reason and explain the reason providing facts and details.

_____

_____

_____

Paragraph 3: State your second reason and explain the reason providing facts and details.

_____

_____

_____

Paragraph 4: State your third reason and explain the reason providing facts and details.

_____

_____

_____

Paragraph 5: Write a conclusion restating your opinion and restating the reasons.

_____

_____

_____

☐ I can use words, phrases, and clauses to connect an opinion and reasons.
☐ I can write a conclusion related to an opinion.

Use the editing checklist to produce a final copy of your opinion essay (pages 69 and 70). Type your final draft on a computer or write it on another sheet of paper. Attach your first draft and this editing sheet to your final draft. Then, have another person read your essay and complete the bottom part of this sheet.

Plan

_____ I have made a written plan that outlines my opinion, my audience, the reasons for my opinion, and facts and details that support the reasons.

Revise

_____ I have written an introductory paragraph that states my opinion.

_____ I have written a closing paragraph that summarizes my opinion.

_____ I have revised my writing for clarity.

_____ I used transition words and phrases to connect my writing.

Edit

_____ I used words correctly.

_____ I have written complete sentences.

_____ I have edited my writing for capitalization and punctuation.

_____ I have edited my writing for spelling errors.

Publish

_____ I have asked someone to read my essay.

The following is to be completed by the reader:

I have read this essay. (signature)_____

I agree / disagree (circle one) with the opinion in this essay because

_____

_____

☐ I can plan, revise, and edit my writing.
☐ I can use technology to create, publish, and show my writing.
☐ I can write over different time frames for various purposes and audiences.

Name_____

Prepare to write a report about something you are studying in science or social studies. Work with your teacher to choose a topic. Use the graphic organizer to help you plan and organize your writing.

Topic

Subtopic 1	Subtopic 2	Subtopic 2

Special Topic Key Words	Special Text Features (maps, charts, etc.)

☐ I can organize my writing and use text features to help readers better understand a topic.
☐ I can use specific information such as facts, definitions, and details to support a topic.
☐ I can use specific words related to the topic to support my writing.

Before writing your report (page 72), research information about the topic. Use a book, the Internet, or other reference materials to gather information. Take notes on your topic.

Topic:

Subtopic 1:
Fact:
Fact:
Source:

Subtopic 2:
Fact:
Fact:
Source:

Subtopic 3:
Fact:
Fact:
Source:

☐ I can research different aspects of a topic using several sources.
☐ I can gather and summarize information and provide sources.
☐ I can use grade-level reading strategies when writing about informational texts.

Use the following format to organize the first draft of your research report (pages 72 and 73). Use words and phrases to connect the ideas throughout your report.

Title: _____

Introductory Paragraph: State your topic, why you chose the topic, and general information about the topic.

_____

_____

_____

Subtopic 1 Heading: _____
State the main idea of subtopic 1 and at least three supporting details.

_____

_____

_____

Subtopic 2 Heading: _____
State the main idea of subtopic 2 and at least three supporting details.

_____

_____

_____

Subtopic 3 Heading: _____
State the main idea of subtopic 3 and at least three supporting details.

_____

_____

_____

Concluding Paragraph: Summarize the information from the report.

_____

_____

_____

☐ I can use words, phrases, and clauses to connect ideas throughout my writing.
☐ I can write a conclusion related to the topic.

Use the editing checklist to produce a final copy of your research report (page 74).

Plan

_____ I have made a written plan that outlines the topic, three subtopics, and key words.

Revise

_____ I have written an introductory paragraph that states my topic and why I chose it.

_____ I have written a closing paragraph that summarizes the information in my report.

_____ I have revised my writing to include key words that are defined in context in my report.

_____ I used transition words and phrases to connect my writing.

Edit

_____ I used words correctly.

_____ I have written complete sentences.

_____ I have edited my writing for capitalization and punctuation.

_____ I have edited my writing for spelling errors.

Publish

_____ I have decided how I will publish and share my report.

☐ I can plan, revise, and edit my writing.
☐ I can write over different time frames for various purposes and audiences.

Use a conjunction from the word bank to combine each pair of simple sentences. Then, write the new sentences. You may use a conjunction more than once.

although	and	because	but	or	so	while

1. Sarah wanted to go swimming. It rained. _____

_____

2. The car broke down. I took a taxi. _____

_____

3. The man was tired. The man sat on a bench. _____

_____

4. It started raining. I opened my umbrella. _____

_____

5. I watered the plant. It wilted. _____

_____

6. The baby cried. The baby was hungry. _____

_____

7. Jeremy bought some milk. He still had some left. _____

_____

8. The boy started a new painting. His first painting was drying. _____

_____

☐ **I can understand when and where to use conjunctions, prepositions, and interjections.**

Underline the interjection in each sentence.

1. Well, we are learning about Egyptian pyramids.

2. Wow, the first pyramid was built in 2780 BC.

3. Yes, we read about the Great Pyramid at Giza.

4. Phew, the Great Pyramid spans 13 acres of land!

5. No, I didn't know that it stands near the Sphinx.

Complete each sentence using an interjection from the word bank. Be sure to include commas as necessary.

| Great | Hey | Wait | Wow | Yes |

6. _____ our room looks like ancient Egypt!

7. _____ we decorated the room for our Egyptian feast.

8. _____ Anna forgot the grapes.

9. _____ I have some we can use.

10. _____ we can use those for our feast.

☐ **I can understand when and where to use conjunctions, prepositions, and interjections.**
☐ **I can use commas when setting off introductory words.**

Underline the preposition in each sentence.

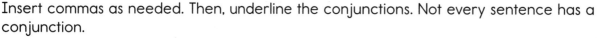

1. The sun shines in our universe.

2. Many planets revolve around the sun.

3. Our planet has one moon in its orbit.

4. The moon orbits near Earth.

5. The *Phoenix* landed on Mars.

6. Sometimes, you can see Venus at night.

7. Jupiter is the largest planet in the solar system.

8. Mercury is the closest planet to our sun.

Insert commas as needed. Then, underline the conjunctions. Not every sentence has a conjunction.

9. Wow there is a lot to learn about the solar system.

10. Our group made models of Mars Earth and Venus.

11. Oh no our models of Earth and Venus fell apart but the model of Mars is fine.

12. Jeremy would you like to travel to Mars or Venus some day?

13. The planets moons and stars are part of the solar system.

14. Don't you think this has been an interesting unit Robert?

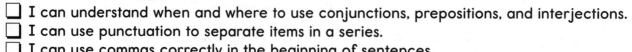

☐ I can understand when and where to use conjunctions, prepositions, and interjections.
☐ I can use punctuation to separate items in a series.
☐ I can use commas correctly in the beginning of sentences.
☐ I can use commas when setting off introductory words or phrases in a sentence.

Name_____

Write the perfect tense of each verb.

	Present Perfect	Past Perfect	Future Perfect
1. walk	_____	_____	_____
2. run	_____	_____	_____
3. jump	_____	_____	_____
4. skip	_____	_____	_____
5. hop	_____	_____	_____
6. join	_____	_____	_____

Complete each sentence with the correct perfect tense of the verb in parentheses.

7. By Friday, the dancers _____ the difficult dance steps. (learn)

8. The dancers _____ difficult dance steps for many performances. (learn)

9. The dancers _____ difficult dance steps before these steps. (learn)

☐ **I can form and use the perfect verb tenses to convey various times, sequences, states, and conditions.**

Circle the incorrect verb in each sentence. Rewrite the sentence using the correct verb tense.

1. Scientists have learn that rhinoceroses have lived on Earth for about 40 million years.

   _____

2. Fossils showing that there were more than 30 species of rhinos.

   _____

3. A rhinoceros ranking as one of the largest land creatures.

   _____

4. Most wild rhinos will live in Africa, southeastern Asia, and Sumatra.

   _____

5. Indian rhinos had skin that looks like a suit of armor.

   _____

6. They inhabiting marshy jungles among reeds and tall grasses.

   _____

7. Illegal hunters, called poachers, have hunt rhinos for their valuable horns for many years.

   _____

8. Some people grinds up rhino horns to treat sicknesses.

   _____

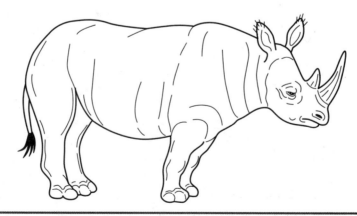

☐ **I can recognize and correct inappropriate shifts in verb tense.**

Complete each sentence with a correlative conjunction (either/or, neither/nor, both/and).

1. _____ James _____ Ryan like the Red Sox baseball team.

2. _____ James _____ Ryan play for the White Sox.

3. James _____ plays first base, _____ he plays outfield.

4. _____ James _____ Ryan got up to bat in the first inning.

5. Unfortunately, _____ James _____ Ryan got a hit.

6. However, in the third inning, _____ James _____ Ryan got hits.

7. _____ Ryan _____ James will sit out the fourth inning to let Sam play.

8. _____ Ryan _____ James like sitting out.

9. _____ James _____ Ryan like to win.

10. After the game, the team will celebrate by going out for _____ pizza

_____ burgers.

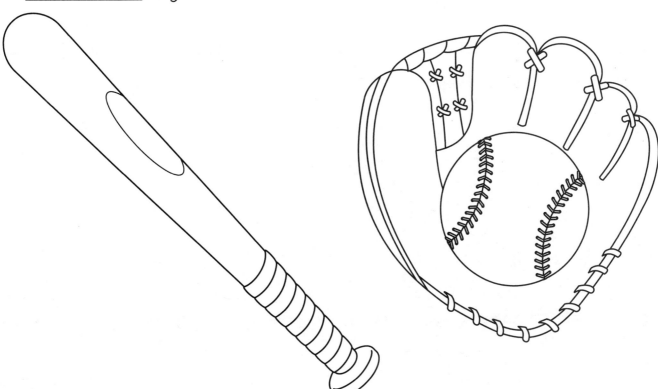

☐ I can use correlative conjunctions such as *either/or* and *neither/nor*.

Rewrite each sentence, inserting commas to separate items in a series.

1. Hayden ordered lasagna salad and milk for dinner.

_____

2. Hayden likes zucchini, but he does not like beans peas or spinach.

_____

3. Hayden couldn't decide whether to have the chocolate strawberry or vanilla yogurt for dessert.

_____

4. Peaches pears and grapes are my favorite fruits.

_____

5. Which do you like most, peaches pears or grapes?

_____

6. My mother made a fruit salad with apples bananas strawberries and grapes.

_____

7. Nicole Marisa and I enjoyed eating the fruit salad.

_____

☐ I can use punctuation to separate items in a series.

Rewrite each sentence, inserting commas to set off an introductory phrase or to indicate direct address.

1. Because my dad was a Boy Scout our family lives by the motto, "Be prepared."

_____

2. Until my sister is a little older my parents will not take us to the amusement park.

_____

3. Before we leave to go anywhere we lock the door to our house.

_____

4. After hearing about the fire at our neighbor's house my family made an emergency plan.

_____

5. Because my cousin is allergic to peanuts we cannot have peanuts in our home.

_____

6. Yes my family must arrive at the airport at least two hours before our flight leaves.

_____

7. Although I think my family is a bit too cautious I appreciate the care they have for me.

_____

8. Is your family as cautious as my family Claire?

_____

9. Jose you will have to leave by seven o'clock.

_____

10. Will I get a good grade Mr. Lee?

_____

☐ **I can use commas correctly in the beginning of sentences.**
☐ **I can use commas when setting off introductory words and phrases and to indicate direct address.**

Write each story title correctly.

  1. The Ugly Duckling _____

  2. The Lion's Share_____

  3. The Fir Tree _____

Write each poem title correctly.

  4. Shooting Stars_____

  5. Always Wondering _____

  6. Floradora Doe _____

Write each song title correctly.

  7. Down in the Valley _____

  8. Go Tell Aunt Rhody _____

  9. Monster Mash_____

Rewrite each sentence, correctly punctuating the titles of works.

10. Our class read the story, The Golden Touch.

_____

11. We sang the Star Spangled Banner at the baseball game.

_____

12. I memorized the entire poem, Paul Revere's Ride.

_____

☐ **I can use appropriate punctuation when writing titles of works.**

Cross out each misspelled word. Then, write the word correctly above the misspelled word. Use a dictionary if needed. There are 12 misspelled words.

Best Friends

Kelly, Aaron, Brandon, and I are best freinds. We are in the same class at school. We have so much fun when we are together. We wanted to go to the movies, so we asked our parents. After our parents agreed to take us, we decided on a movie and made plans to meet at the theater Saturday afternoon. Kelly arrived first, and Aaron and Brandon arrived imediatly after. As usual, I was late. By the time I got their, every one was in line to buy snacks. They knew better than to wait for me. Brandon ordered nachos, popcorn, and a large lemonade. I could not beleive that he planned to eat so much. "I'm a growing boy," Brandon always said. The rest of us decided to share a large pop corn. Then, it was time to find our seats. The theater was so dark we couldn't see any thing. We stumbled in and sat in the first row. Luckily, the theater was empty becuz we spent the entire time whispering and giggleing. I could not even tell you what the movie was about. After it ended, our parents picked us up. We said goodby and headed home. If our parents agree, we will get together agin next weekend and go bowling. Its fun to have best friends.

❑ **I can spell words correctly and use reference materials when necessary.**

A fifth grader might say "Hi! How are you?" when she greets a friend. Draw a line to another way to say this phrase to the person who might say it.

1. "Yo, man, what's happening?"   A. someone from the South

2. "Hello, my dear. How have you been?"   B. cool dude

3. "Hey, y'all, what y'all doing?"   C. grumpy old man

4. "Hi, how's it going?"   D. sweet old lady

5. "Umph. What's a matter with you?"   E. mother

Write the same sentence in three different ways to convey the emotions in parentheses.

6. (excitement)

_____

_____

7. (disappointment)

_____

_____

8. (surprise)

_____

_____

☐ I can create sentences to convey various meanings.
☐ I can compare and contrast varieties of English in written works.

Name_____

Match the words in the first column with the definitions in the second column. Each word will have more than one definition. Use a dictionary if needed.

1. palm _____

2. fiddle _____

3. court _____

4. vessel _____

5. mask _____

6. harp _____

7. prompt _____

8. sore _____

9. glare _____

10. cabinet_____

A. a tube in the body

B. a stringed instrument played with a bow

C. to dwell on a subject

D. angry

E. flat part of the hand

F. a face used for disguise

G. a harsh, bright light

H. move hands and fingers restlessly

I. tender, painful

J. cupboard

K. on time

L. enclosed playing area

M. to assist an actor by saying his next words

N. type of tree

O. a stringed instrument played by plucking

P. a large boat

Q. stare angrily

R. a place where judges hear cases

S. advisers to the president

T. to cover up; hide something

☐ I can use reference materials to learn about unfamiliar words and phrases.
☐ I can use relationships between words to better understand each of the words.

Write the word that is the antonym of the other words. Use a dictionary if needed.

1. old	elderly	young	antique	aged	_____
2. chuckle	laugh	snicker	sigh	giggle	_____
3. screen	hide	conceal	cover	view	_____
4. mend	repair	fix	rip	patch	_____
5. cry	weep	laugh	sob	wail	_____
6. beautiful	stunning	hideous	gorgeous		_____
7. kind	pleasant	agreeable	unsociable		_____
8. tight	stretched	loose	taut		_____

Circle the synonym in parentheses for the bold word in each sentence.

9. We were **floating** down the river on our inner tubes. (gliding, sailing)

10. I was so **excited** about going to the beach that I could not sleep. (enthusiastic, nervous)

11. My brother **collects** autographs of movie stars. (gathers, finds)

12. Whitney has been **late** to class several times this year. (tardy, slow)

13. Jose needed a **plain** sheet of paper to draw his picture. (simple, ordinary)

14. Our class needs to inflate 50 balloons for the **celebration**. (party, parade)

15. Could I have a **piece** of your delicious apple pie? (section, slice)

16. Our class **constructed** a model of the solar system. (built, saw)

☐ **I can use relationships between words to better understand each of the words.**

Write the adjective or adverb in parentheses that makes each sentence clearer and more interesting.

1. The concert hall was _____. (nice, fabulous)

2. It was _____ decorated in red and gold velvet. (handsomely, neatly)

3. The audience waited _____ for the concert to begin. (eagerly, happily)

4. The _____ conductor raised his baton. (talented, good)

5. The _____ orchestra came to attention. (big, huge)

6. The audience was _____ still. (very, absolutely)

7. The orchestra performed _____. (well, magnificently)

8. The tenor sang _____. (nicely, brilliantly)

9. The audience clapped _____. (enthusiastically, loudly)

10. It was a _____ concert. (splendid, good)

Underline the adjective or adverb in parentheses that makes each phrase clearer and more interesting.

11. a harp's (nice, delicate) tones

12. reacted (joyously, nicely)

13. a (difficult, hard) composition

14. (good, outstanding) performance

15. sang (well, beautifully)

16. played (remarkably, nicely)

17. a (world-famous, good) orchestra

18. performed (successfully, well)

☐ **I can create sentences to convey various meanings.**

Draw a line to match each idiom with its meaning.

1. Who let the cat out of the bag?

2. Can I add my two cents?

3. Don't cry over spilled milk.

4. Mark is a chip off the old block.

5. Nick is the apple of his mother's eye.

6. Julio can do that with one hand tied behind his back.

A. Don't worry about something that cannot be changed.

B. He can do it easily.

C. Can I give my opinion?

D. He is special.

E. He is like his father.

F. Who told the secret?

Draw a line to match the proverb or adage with its meaning.

7. A stitch in time saves nine.

8. Live and learn.

9. If at first you don't succeed, try, try again.

10. Slow and steady wins the race.

11. The early bird catches the worm.

12. Don't judge a book by its cover.

G. Keep working toward the goal.

H. Take time to fix something before it becomes a big problem.

I. Don't make a decision about something or someone by what you see on the outside.

J. Learn from your mistakes.

K. Don't give up because you make a mistake.

L. It is better to do things early than to put them off.

☐ I can recognize and explain idioms, adages, and proverbs.

Answer Key

Page 12
1. row of trees and soldiers standing at attention; Answers will vary. 2. cars and ants crawling along; Answers will vary. 3. clowns and sardines packed; Answers will vary. 4. shadows and ghosts dancing; Answers will vary; 5. sound of waves lapping and a dog getting a drink; Answers will vary; 6. baseball flew and rocket; Answers will vary.

Page 13
1. by a lake; "they had to shower because they were muddy" or "went back to the lake"; 2. for a long weekend; "three pairs of shorts, three T-shirts"; 3. eat fish they caught; "they placed their. . . fishing gear" or "went back to the lake with their poles and bait"; 4. lake; "they had to shower because they were muddy"

Page 15
1. C; 2. Answers will vary, but possible answers include that the word shadow is used at the end of the third line of each stanza. *Eldorado* is used as the last word in each stanza. The rhyme scheme is aabccb. 3. Answers will vary, but possible answers include: for the rhythm and rhyme; to make it easier to read and understand. 4. He dies; "as his strength failed him at length"; 5. Answers will vary, but possible answers

include that Poe might have been suggesting that people should pursue their dreams no matter how long it takes them, or that people should appreciate what they have and not waste their lives seeking unattainable treasures.

Page 17
1. Answers will vary, but possible answers include that a brave boy places his finger in a hole in a dike to keep the water from bursting through the dike and flooding the town. 2. A dike is a wall that holds back water. 3. Answers will vary. 4. B; 5. the voice of the ocean murmuring

Page 19
1. Answers will vary, but possible answers include that an old man set the town's rice fields on fire to save the people of the town from a tsunami. 2. Answers will vary, but possible answers include: Similarities: The main characters bravely act alone to save the townspeople. Water is a powerful, destructive force. Differences: "The Hero of Harlem" has a young boy as a main character and the setting of a dike in Holland. "The Burning of the Rice Fields" has an old man as a main character and the setting of rice fields in Japan.

Page 21
1. Answers will vary, but possible answers may include that Finlay and Murchadh are both kind. Finlay is young and Murchadh is old. 2. Finlay moves from one relative's home to another. Murchadh has lived in his home for a long time. 3. B; "Long ago" indicates it is not present day. The setting indicates it is not thousands or millions of years ago. 4. Answers will vary, but possible answers include being found by a kind shepherd.

Page 23
1. Answers will vary, but possible answers include that an orphan finds good fortune after being taken in by a kind shepherd and sleeping in a yew tree. 2. A;
3.

Folk Tale Characteristics	"The Hero of Harlem"	"The Yew Tree"
Ordinary Characters	a young boy	an orphan; a shepherd
Storyteller's Beginning	long ago	long ago
A Problem to Solve	hole in a dike	an unloved orphan
A Happy Ending	A boy saves the town.	An orphan finds gold and a home with a kind shepherd.
A Positive Theme	No one is too young to help.	Good things happen to good people.

Page 25
1. Jess; 2. the pronoun *I* and the conversations; 3. Jess and Jim are siblings and are

Answer Key

adventurous. Jess is younger and more cautious. Jim is older and brave. 4. Answers will vary, but possible answers include that the dialogue would be different, and the reader would know more of Jim's thoughts. 5. fast-moving river

Page 27
1. Jess becomes brave to help Jim. 2. Answers will vary. 3. Answers will vary. 4. Answers will vary, but possible answers include knowing more about Jim's thoughts or the pain Jim was in. 5. Answers will vary, but possible answers include being able to know more about what each of the characters were thinking.

Page 28
1. Laws are rules that help people live together. 2. Traffic laws keep people safe on the roads. Police officers enforce laws. Laws protect people's freedoms. 3. to protect the rights of all citizens

Page 29
1. F; 2. F; 3. T; 4. T; 5. F

Page 31
1. nonfiction; real-life story; 2. She was awarded the Nobel Prize. She and her husband became known worldwide for their work studying radioactivity. 3. B; 4. Answers will vary, but possible events on the time line include: born

on November 7, 1867; went to college in 1891; graduated in 1893; earned a second degree in 1894; married in 1895; died on July 4, 1934.

Page 33
1. He discovered a way to control silkworm disease. He developed vaccines. He developed the process of pasteurization. 2. a doctor; 3. People who earn advanced degrees are called doctors. 4. Answers will vary, but possible answers include yes, because they lived in France during the same time. 5. Answers will vary, but possible events on the time line include: Pasteur: born in 1822; opened a research center in 1888; died in 1895. Sklodowska: born in 1867; died in 1934.

Page 35
1. Answers will vary, but possible answers include the author thinks they are beautiful because he uses words like *delight, colorful,* and *beautiful.* 2. Answers will vary, but possible answers include pollution, littering, and overuse of oceans. 3. like a busy city; like tiny flowers; 4. Answers will vary.

Page 37
1. It is difficult to determine the truth of events from the past. 2. People see things in different ways. Newspaper

reports can present one side of an event. Events can be complicated. 3. You have to gather evidence from many different sources to discover the truth of what happened. 4. Answers will vary, but possible answers include talking to people who were there and studying artifacts. 5. Answers will vary.

Page 39
1. Chinese immigrants were treated unfairly in the late 1800s and early 1900s. 2. C; 3. G; 4. E; 5. F; 6. H; 7. D; 8. A; 9. B

Page 41
1. Chinese immigration in the early 1900s; 2. to inform the reader about the unfair treatment of Chinese immigrants; 3. Answers will vary, but possible answers may include that both passages tell that Angel Island was an immigration station for Chinese immigrants beginning in 1910. 4. Answers will vary, but possible answers may include "Immigration at Angel Island" provides more information about the discrimination of the Chinese immigrants through the Chinese Exclusion Act. 5. Answers will vary, but possible answers may include *Poems from Angel Island* includes information about how the Chinese immigrants felt about being detained on Angel Island.

Answer Key

Page 43
1. Answers will vary, but possible events on the time line include: saw first airplane in 1907; saw a stunt-flying exhibition in 1917; took flying lessons in 1921; 2. Answers will vary. 3. Answers will vary.

Page 45
1. He was an explorer of the western frontier and a fur trapper. (Students should include evidence from text to support their answers.) 2. Answers will vary, but possible answers include that they were both legendary, brave, and adventurous. 3. Answers will vary, but possible answers include that both passages are organized under subheadings. 4. The headings in "A Pioneer of Flight" are organized chronologically; in "John Colter: Western Explorer," the headings are organized by topic.

Page 47
Answers will vary.

Page 48
1. Answers will vary. 2. as if bragging or boasting; 3 A. arrogant: boastful; B. humble: modest; 4. taunted; 5. turtle

Page 49
1. Answers will vary. 2. sweetly; 3. Don't be proud. 4. bird

Page 51
1. Answers will vary. 2. Answers will vary, but possible answers include reading quietly.

3.

Descriptions of the White Owl	Descriptions of Winter
eyes shine darkly	quiet moon at midnight
downy feathers	snow falls gently
floats from tree to limb	moon casts her pale light
Owl is alone.	Nature is in silent slumber.

4. like the downy feathers;
5. Answers will vary.

Page 53
1. A; 2. Answers will vary, but possible answers include: bit an angle-worm in halves, ate the fellow, drank a dew, hopped sidewise, glanced with rapid eyes, stirred his velvet head, unrolled his feathers. 3. flew away; 4. rowed home like a boat on an ocean

Page 54
1. Everyone is good at something. 2. a special skill; 3. talent, flair, skill, gift; 4. C

Page 55
1. Monkeys and apes are primates. 2. They have complex brains. They use their front limbs as hands. They can use tools. 3. Answers will vary, but possible answers include *primary, prime, primitive*. 4. complex; not simple, with parts; 5. human; Answers will vary, but possible answers include *humane, humanity, humble*; 6. chim-pan-zee

Page 56
1. me-dul-la; part of the brain that controls involuntary actions; 2. cer-e-bel-lum; part of the brain that controls the voluntary actions; 3. ce-re-brum; part of the brain that controls the voluntary mental operations; 4. in-vol-un-tary; actions that do not require decision making; 5. vol-un-tary; actions that require instruction

Page 57
1. Answers will vary. 2A. pre-his-tor-ic; before history; B. civ-i-li-za-tion; a human society; C. ar-chae-ol-o-gist; one who studies ancient things; D. an-ces-tral; having to do with ancestors; 3. Answers will vary, but possible answers include in a book about the Anasazi or a social studies textbook. 4. Answers will vary, but possible answers include for a report or to learn more about their culture.

Page 58
1. atmosphere; 2. launched; 3. evaluated; 4. mission; 5. transformed; 6. distorts; 7. former; 8. theories; 9. universe; 10. payloads; 11. Sputnik I

Answer Key

Page 59
1. classmates; 2. Answers will vary, but possible answers include special activities or privileges. 3. Answers will vary, but possible answers may include getting new textbooks. 4. Answers will vary.

Page 60
Answers will vary, but possible answers are included below.

Did you know that you can plant a sunflower seed inside a cup? It is simple and fun! **First**, gather the following materials: a clear, plastic cup; a wet paper towel; and a sunflower seed. **Next**, place the paper towel inside the cup. **At this point**, make sure that the paper towel covers the entire inside of the cup. Place the seed on the paper towel and fold the paper towel over the seed. **Then**, place the cup near a window with a lot of sunlight shining through. If your sunflower does not get enough sunlight, it will not be able to grow. It will take three weeks for your seed to sprout. **In the meantime**, you can record any changes that you observe. **Finally**, you will be able to see your sunflower flourish.

Page 61
Answers will vary.

Page 62
1. Answers will vary, but possible descriptions may include cold, musty, drafty, or chilly. 2. Answers will vary, but possible descriptions may include bright, tall, quiet, or worn down. 3. Answers will vary, but possible descriptions may include colorful, aromatic, fresh, or beautiful.
4. Answers will vary, but possible descriptions may include tight, squishy, smelly, or hot.

Page 63
1. Answers will vary. 2. Answers will vary.

Page 64
1. Answers will vary. 2. Answers will vary. 3. Answers will vary. 4. Answer will vary.

Page 65
Answers will vary.

Page 66
Setting: Dike in Harlem, Holland; Characters: Hans, his younger brother, the townspeople; Problem: There was a hole in the dike. Event 1: Hans put his finger in the hole. Event 2: Hans's brother ran to get help. Event 3: The townspeople came. Solution: The dike was fixed and Hans was a hero.

Page 67
Answers will vary.

Page 68
Answers will vary.

Page 69
Answers will vary.

Page 70
Answers will vary.

Page 71
Answers will vary.

Page 72
Answers will vary.

Page 73
Answers will vary.

Page 74
Answers will vary.

Page 75
Answers will vary.

Page 76
1. Sarah wanted to go swimming, but it rained. 2. The car broke down, so I took a taxi. 3. The man was tired, so he sat on a bench. 4. It started raining, so I opened my umbrella. 5. I watered the plant, but it wilted. 6. The baby cried because she was hungry. 7. Jeremy bought some milk although he still had some left. 8. The boy started a new painting while his first painting was drying.

Page 77
1. Well,; 2. Wow,; 3. Yes,; 4. Phew,; 5. No,; 6. Wow,; 7. Yes,; 8. Wait,; 9. Hey,; 10. Great,

Page 78
1. in; 2. around; 3. in; 4. near;

94

Answer Key

5. on; 6. at; 7. in; 8. to; 9. Wow, there is a lot to learn about the solar system. 10. Our group made models of Mars, Earth, and Venus. 11. Oh no, our models of Earth and Venus fell apart, but the model of Mars is fine. 12. Jeremy, would you like to travel to Mars or Venus some day? 13. The planets, moons, and stars are part of the solar system. 14. Don't you think this has been an interesting unit, Robert?

Page 79
1. have/has walked, had walked, will have walked; 2. have/has run, had run, will have run; 3. have/has jumped, had jumped, will have jumped; 4. have/has skipped, had skipped, will have skipped; 5. have/has hopped, had hopped, will have hopped; 6. have/has joined, had joined, will have joined; 7. will have learned; 8. have learned; 9. had learned

Page 80
1. Scientists have learned that rhinoceroses have lived on Earth for about 40 million years. 2. Fossils show that there were more than 30 species of rhinos. 3. A rhinoceros ranks as one of the largest land creatures. 4. Most wild rhinos live in Africa, southeastern Asia, and Sumatra. 5. Indian rhinos have skin that looks like a suit of armor. 6. They inhabit marshy jungles among reeds and tall grasses. 7. Illegal hunters, called poachers, have hunted rhinos for their valuable horns for many years. 8. Some people grind up rhino horns to treat sicknesses.

Page 81
1. Neither/nor; 2. Both/and; 3. either/or; 4. Both/and; 5. neither/nor; 6. both/and; 7. Either/or; 8. Neither/nor; 9. Both/and; 10. either/or

Page 82
1. Hayden ordered lasagna, salad, and milk for dinner. 2. Hayden likes zucchini, but he does not like beans, peas, or spinach. 3. Hayden couldn't decide whether to have the chocolate, strawberry, or vanilla yogurt for dessert. 4. Peaches, pears, and grapes are my favorite fruits. 5. Which do you like most, peaches, pears, or grapes? 6. My mother made a fruit salad with apples, bananas, strawberries, and grapes. 7. Nicole, Marisa, and I enjoyed eating the fruit salad.

Page 83
1. Because my dad was a Boy Scout, our family lives by the motto, "Be prepared." 2. Until my sister is a little older, my parents will not take us to the amusement park. 3. Before we leave to go anywhere, we lock the door to our house. 4. After hearing about the fire at our neighbor's house, my family made an emergency plan. 5. Because my cousin is allergic to peanuts, we cannot have peanuts in our home. 6. Yes, my family must arrive at the airport at least two hours before our flight leaves. 7. Although I think my family is a bit too cautious, I appreciate the care they have for me. 8. Is your family as cautious as my family, Claire? 9. Jose, you will have to leave by seven o'clock. 10. Will I get a good grade, Mr. Lee?

Page 84
1. "The Ugly Duckling"; 2. "The Lion's Share"; 3. "The Fir Tree"; 4. "Shooting Stars"; 5. "Always Wondering"; 6. "Floradora Doe"; 7. "Down in the Valley"; 8. "Go Tell Aunt Rhody"; 9. "Monster Mash"; 10. Our class read the story, "The Golden Touch." 11. We sang the "Star-Spangled Banner" at the baseball game. 12. I memorized the entire poem "Paul Revere's Ride."

Answer Key

Page 85

Kelly, Aaron, Brandon, and I are best **friends**. We are in the same class at school. We have so much fun when we are together. We wanted to go to the movies, so we asked our parents. After our parents agreed to take us, we decided on a movie and made plans to meet at the theater Saturday afternoon. Kelly arrived first; and Aaron and Brandon arrived **immediately** after. As usual, I was late. By the time I got **there, everyone** was in line to buy snacks. They knew better than to wait for me. Brandon ordered nachos, popcorn, and a large lemonade. I could not **believe** that he planned to eat so much. "I'm a growing boy," Brandon always said. The rest of us decided to share a large **popcorn**. Then it was time to find our seats. The theater was so dark we couldn't see **anything**. We stumbled in and sat in the first row. Luckily, the theater was empty **because** we spent the entire time whispering and **giggling**. I could not even tell you what the movie was about. After it ended, our parents picked us up. We said **good-bye** and headed home. If our parents agree, we will get together **again** next weekend and go bowling. **It's** fun to have best friends.

Page 86

1. B; 2. D; 3. A; 4. E; 5. C;
6–8. Answers will vary.

Page 87

1. E, N; 2. B, H; 3. L, R; 4. A, P;
5. F, T; 6. C, O; 7. K, M; 8. D, L;
9. G, Q; 10. J, S

Page 88

1. young; 2. sigh; 3. view;
4. rip; 5. laugh; 6. hideous;
7. unsociable; 8. loose;
9. gliding; 10. enthusiastic;
11. gathers; 12. tardy;
13. ordinary; 14. party; 15. slice;
16. built

Page 89

1. fabulous; 2. handsomely;
3. eagerly; 4. talented; 5. huge;
6. absolutely; 7. magnificently;
8. brilliantly; 9. enthusiastically;
10. splendid; 11. delicate;
12. joyously; 13. difficult;
14. outstanding; 15. beautifully;
16. remarkably; 17. world-famous; 18. successfully

Page 90

1. F; 2. C; 3. A; 4. E; 5. D; 6. B;
7. H; 8. J; 9. K; 10. G; 11. L; 12. I